MW01289906

RETIRING EARLY, SIMPLIFYING MY LIFE, AND REALIZING THAT LESS IS BEST

Jen Beck Seymour

FOR MY GREG

I wouldn't be where I am today without you,
and I can't go where I want tomorrow without you.

Table of Contents

PART I – DREAMING THE DREAM

1. the beginning of the end

"I QUIT!!"

Uh, oh.

I had glanced at my phone briefly when it vibrated and lit up with my husband's text. I was at work, in my windowless cubicle, surrounded by brown expandable file folders smelling heavily of stale paper and spilled coffee. My hands still on my keyboard, I was in the middle of typing a long metes and bounds legal description that was needed in 20 minutes.

I knew Greg didn't mean that he actually had quit his job, but that he was at his wits end, and ready to give his notice at any moment. My heart sank. It was another bad day for him, which was becoming more and more frequent lately. Greg was a leader in a dying business, and he managed both the sales and production departments. He constantly had to handle the individual personalities and temperaments of these disparate groups. In addition to these two groups, he also had to constantly deal with the demands of working with his clients, attorneys and paralegals. Greg's job sucked. There was no other way to put it.

I texted him back a quick message, "Hang in there, babe. I love you," knowing it was lame, but I was in the middle of a stressful day myself, not to mention the urgent legal description that was now needed in 18 minutes, and quite frankly, I didn't have time for this.

Throughout the rest of the afternoon, between various projects, I brainstormed on things I could do for him that night that might cheer him up a bit. We had been married for almost 17 years, and I still took pride in being a darn good wife.

In the past, I would do any number of tiny little things that would make his night that much better: fix him a nice dinner; stop and get his favorite take-out; pick up some beer; or, you know... . However, it seemed like this was becoming a daily dilemma. In fact, wasn't it just yesterday I had picked up a 6-pack of Fat Tire beer for him on my way home from work?

So on my drive home, after my own taxing day, I found myself totally and utterly exhausted, both mentally and physically, and feeling just a wee bit selfish. After all, who is to say I hadn't experienced a grueling, stressful day as well?

I ended up doing *nothing* for Greg. I drove straight home, not even sure if we had anything I could throw together for dinner. All I could think about was changing into my comfy yoga pants and T-shirt, scraping my hair up into a pony-tail, pouring myself a glass of wine, lounging on the couch, and reading my latest "chick lit" book (translation: no sex tonight).

I felt horrible!

This was my life – and it had been like this for the previous two years. I knew it was getting to Greg more than me. But it was also starting to take a toll on our marriage. We were both so drained all the time, that more often than not we had exhausted all efforts of taking care of each other. When one of us really seemed to need it, the other was too busy, or too stressed out, or working late, and we just weren't able to 'be there' for each other. It was getting to be too exhausting.

And we don't even have kids! I mean, what kind of a marriage is it when you can't take care of each other in times of need? Greg was usually either too wiped out or not available to be there for me when I needed him, and I was tired of not being able to make things better for him when he needed me. I hated feeling helpless.

We had become deeply entrenched in the North American philosophy that "more is better." We were busy all the time making more and having more, but if you asked me exactly what I was busy *with* all the time, I couldn't have told you. Meaningless busy-ness – the worst kind of busy.

In our case, Greg's job was slowly and literally draining the life out of him, out of both of us. He had been on medication for high blood pressure for over a year. We both had reverted to eating horribly – going out to dinner all the time and eating awful junk food. We couldn't seem to stop the downward spiral of being stressed out and unhealthy.

I didn't hate my job necessarily, but I sometimes would ask myself, "What exactly am I doing with my life?" I had grown up playing piano, and then later studied psychology in college, but somehow had ended up in the commercial title insurance business. Instead of becoming a concert pianist or a psychologist, I was sitting in an artificially lit cubicle all day. It was a well-paying and respectable job, but sometimes I would get introspective and would think things like: what do I *really* do all day, except shuffle paper around and do a lot of computer work (which would result in more shuffling of paper), all to ensure that businesses properly own a piece of land and have legal title to it?

Don't get me wrong – I know commercial title insurance is important and necessary. Only it didn't really make me feel *good* about myself at the end of the day. It was a job, one at which I was accomplished, but a job nonetheless which only served to pay the bills.

I had several hobbies and activities which made me happy and helped me to not define myself by my job: baking, playing piano, reading, painting, calligraphy, and running. Greg didn't have time for his hobbies anymore. Our marriage and our happiness, which were important to both of us, seemed to be at stake.

In addition to worrying about Greg, I was starting to get lonely. He would frequently have to return to the office at the most inopportune times. More often than not, I'd be left alone with my dog on what was supposed to be a "date night." We'd be eating out on a Saturday night at a prime spot in the heart of Dallas (Mexican food, if it was Greg's choice), and I'd be dressed up in my designer jeans and high-heeled-wedge sandals. After having waited for a table, we would finally sit down to eat – al fresco, enjoying people-watching and each other's company. And then, two drinks and an appetizer into our evening, Greg's phone would go off, and we'd both literally sink in our chairs. He'd leave the table, make a call, and come back later with a gruff, "I'm going to have to go into work for a bit," – not happy about it, but resigned.

I was resigned too. I mean, I knew there was nothing I could do about it. We would track down our waiter to pay the bill, and then race home; where Greg would drop me off and then head to work for who-knows-how-long.

I respect and enjoy my alone time, trust me, but this was becoming ridiculous.

Then there were the times Greg *was* home with me (or out to dinner with me), but he wasn't really "there", mentally. He would just sit there – staring off into space. I don't know which was worse – not being there physically or not being there mentally.

Something had to give.

2. the beginning of the beginning

Our life wasn't always like this. Before I knew Greg, I knew Richard, Greg's father. I had moved to Dallas from the bitterly cold city of Minneapolis to be with my new fiancé, Michael.

Michael and I had met in Dallas at a friend's wedding and hit it off. Within months we were engaged, and I quit my job in Minneapolis and moved to Dallas. To say my parents were concerned about this development would be an understatement, but I was an independent, mature, 23-year-old woman, so of course I knew what I was doing.

I had gotten a good job within the first week of being in Dallas, had my own apartment (cheap rent!), and was meeting people from my fiancé's church. Since his church, the Church of Christ, was not at all like my Catholic Church I'd known growing up, I started talking to one of the ministers there – "Brother Seymour."

Richard was a very upbeat and happy person. He was also down to earth, objective, a good listener and question answerer, and he knew how to make me feel welcome.

Not wanting to leave the Catholic Church completely behind, I also started going to a Catholic Church in town, which had a huge singles group where I made some more friends. My life was pretty diverse.

One night, Richard and his wife Shirley invited Michael and me over for dinner. *This* was the night I met my future husband.

The clouds did not open up. The angels did not sing. No light bulbs went off. I did not have an "ah-hah!" moment.

Do you think he said one word to me all night? Nope. "Silent Greg" had just moved home from Houston, where his girlfriend had broken up with him and broken his heart. Greg didn't even try to put on a show for us. He was transparent in his grief, sitting at the dinner table, staring at his plate and not saying much of anything until he excused himself. Honestly, I didn't think too much about him at the time as Michael and I were having a good conversation with Richard and Shirley and had a very enjoyable evening.

A few months later, as I was starting to feel more comfortable living in Dallas, I was also starting to feel less comfortable about my relationship with Michael. I hated to admit it, but my parents were right about him. Put another way – I soon came to the conclusion that he wasn't "the guy" for me.

Breaking up is hard to do, especially when you are in a new city and state, and also when the other person doesn't agree with this decision.

After the breaking up was over (this took a couple months), I did not want to "run back home to Mommy and Daddy" and admit defeat. I thought I could stick it out in Dallas for a while longer. I knew it would probably be good for me, and would make me a more well-rounded person. It would let me experience a different way of life, where people said "y'all" and "fixin' " and wore cowboy hats when it wasn't even Halloween.

So… I stayed in Dallas. I made friends from work and my two church singles groups. I enjoyed going on a few casual dates now and then. Life was pretty good.

Then one Sunday after church service, some tall dude in cowboy boots came up to me and said, "Hey, I think we might both work in the same building downtown." It was "Silent Greg!"

We discovered that we did work in the same building, just three floors apart. We chatted for a while (he actually *could* talk!) and ended with an agreement to do lunch sometime.

We met for lunch and continued meeting once a month or so. Slowly, we actually formed a comfortable friendship.

One day, I decided to test our friendship, and so I told him all about this guy I was dating at the time. Hmmmm. Wrong decision. "Silent Greg" was back. He became very quiet, averted his gaze, and changed the subject.

A few months later, I got a better indication of where Greg and I stood. I was currently boyfriend-less, and one day at lunch Greg asked me if I wanted to see a movie. He did it in a way that was perfectly friendly, but also, this was a movie, so of course I knew this had *date potential.* In any case, still not knowing how I really felt about him, I agreed to go.

The time for the date arrived, and "Silent Greg" turned into "No-Show Greg". He stood me up!

Greg had inadvertently scheduled our date for the July 4th holiday. On July 4th, when Greg realized this, he wanted to confirm we were still on for that evening. When he called, and I didn't answer my phone (these were the days before caller-ID), he freaked out, didn't leave a message, and somehow convinced himself that I had forgotten our "date."

The next morning we saw each other in the elevator, and I totally called him out, "Hey! Weren't we supposed to see a movie yesterday?"

He turned beet-red, stuttered around, and mumbled some incoherent apology; all the while with a silly grin on his face. I think he was secretly happy that I hadn't forgotten our "date."

We made plans for another movie night, and this time we made it! He picked me up that night in the "Grey Ghost" (a 1979 grayish-colored Cougar), and we had a lovely dinner at Bennigan's, followed by the movie "The Firm." I let him pay, since he seemed to really want to, and when he walked me up to my apartment door later that night, he took me in his arms and then – he kissed me.

And folks, suddenly, I *did* have my "ah-hah!" moment. The clouds opened up! The angels sang! The fireworks went off! All at once. Wow.

Sure, I've had my share of great kisses, but never had I been so surprised by a kiss – and in a good way! He unexpectedly, and quite literally, swept me off my feet.

We were inseparable from that day forward. A year later we were engaged, and in another six months, married!

3. dreaming of 50 cent beer

Soon after Greg and I had officially started dating, Richard took me aside one day and said, "Jen, I want you to know, that of all my sons, Greg is the romantic one."

I knew this. But now, after all these years, I really know that Greg is truly romantic – and kind, intuitive and, well, just a huge sweetheart.

As well as being romantic, my husband has always been a dreamer. Being a dreamer means you're optimistic, always thinking of different things and new options – thinking for yourself and not just what someone taught you. Dreamers are usually very artistic and romantic, and Greg is all of these things.

Nobody is perfect, however, and we've had some trials and tribulations along the way, but I feel like we have something special that few people have. The older I get, the more I respect him. He makes me feel that I am truly the luckiest girl in the world.

Anyway (now that y'all feel warm and fuzzy), it is not unusual for Greg to tell me his dreams. And by dreams, I don't mean the sleeping kind, but fully awake daytime dreams. I also have learned through the course of our marriage not to get too excited about these dreams or jump up and down and say, "Yes, that's a *great* idea – let's do that right away!" – because, trust me, he would take me at my word and be off implementing said dream in a heartbeat!

It's not unusual for Greg to come home from work and start into a conversation right away with, "Jen, I've been thinking... ," which is when I know to brace myself for a who-knows-what kind of dream. One time he was ready to quit his job and leave me for six months to hike the Appalachian Trail. Granted, that sounded pretty cool (I love hiking too), and he *did* ask me to come with him, but someone had to stay home and pay the bills. Luckily that dream faded away, and I wasn't going to bring it up again. Another time he came home from work and told me all about his plan to quit his job and start a door-to-door mobile dry cleaning service. I was beginning to see a pattern here – all his ideas started with him quitting his job.

Greg and I are good for each other and tend to balance each other out. Sometimes I do go along with his spontaneity and dreams, and we have a blast. But more times than not we end up talking things through, the pros and the cons, and discover that the dream *might* be a good idea, but first, let's see how things pan out and whether we really want to pursue it or not. In other words, maybe if we wait for a while, the dream will be forgotten.

One night, as we were lying in bed, each reading our own book, I asked Greg what he was reading.

He said, "Well, actually it's an e-book by Tim Leffel called *The World's Cheapest Destinations.* It's quite interesting – about the best and cheapest places to live throughout the world."

This didn't faze me at all, knowing what a dreamer he is, but I proceeded to ask him the dutiful-wife question of *why*, and he told me, "I've been researching and reading different articles lately; and maybe, just maybe, this is my way out. *Our* way out. A way for us to retire early and not have to work... ."

I was perking up now. "Really? How could we possibly quit our jobs and not have to work? Not sure I'm following you."

"I know it sounds odd," he said, "but seriously, I think there is a way we could do it. But here's the thing: we can't do it in the United States. The taxes and healthcare are too outrageously expensive here."

"Hmmmmmmm," I replied (which is code for: ARE YOU CRAZY??).

Prior to this point, we had carefully thought through the possibility of Greg quitting his job and taking a job elsewhere or doing something different, but he felt like he would just be trading one stressful management job for another, and he wasn't trained for any other type of industry. He would have to start all over again.

He had thought about starting his own business, but there is always a lot of start-up money needed for that, and also there is always a chance of it failing, as many first-time businesses do. That just seemed too risky at this point in our lives.

Hearing for the first time this "quit our jobs and move to a foreign country" from Greg, I treated it like just another one of his dreams that he is really into at the moment. I felt quite certain it would never come to fruition. I mean, come on! How could we quit our jobs and give up our income at this stage in our lives?

Just for grins, however, and because I didn't want him to think I wasn't taking him seriously, I asked him, "Okay, so where in the world are decent, cheap places to live?"

Greg replied, "It says here that you can get a 50-cent beer in Panama."

"Oh, that's a *great* reason, hon!" (code for: YOU CANNOT BE SERIOUS).

Greg just smiled, ignored my sarcasm, and plugged on, "Look, it says Panama is friendly to Americans, ever since the U.S. finished building the Panama Canal in 1914. The form of currency is the U.S. dollar, and English is widely spoken, although Spanish is the main language. There is also Ecuador – I was just reading that rent and food are supposed to be very cheap there."

"Hmmmmm," I replied again (this time code for: YOU HONESTLY THINK WE COULD DO THIS?).

He told me to just sleep on it for a while.

So, I fell asleep that night dreaming of all the free time I would have from not spending forty-plus hours a week in my little cubicle.

Greg fell asleep dreaming of cheap beer.

4. dream or reality

Every day Greg kept talking about foreign countries and retiring early and quitting his job – and I was forced to listen to him, mainly because my heart did ache for him. I knew he was in a miserable place, and maybe, if we could actually retire early, I needed to listen and start seriously thinking about it myself.

Greg and I have never felt like a "normal" couple exactly. Everyone we knew was following the popular, yuppie plan of having an expensive, showy wedding with 500+ guests, getting a dog, popping out at least two kids and then buying the requisite mini-van and sexy BMW to keep in the garage of their fabulous heavily mortgaged 4000+ square foot home.

We started out on this normal plan, by planning a large and sophisticated wedding. But as the invitee list grew larger and larger, and the money signs got bigger and bigger, we became uneasy. With Greg's family being such a huge part of the Church of Christ, and with us not wanting to leave anyone out, we realized that we would have to invite the whole congregation (which was 'the norm' at this church). Both Greg and I have never liked being the center of attention, and once we discussed it further – we thought, well, we don't HAVE to have a big wedding, right? Let's do the opposite: SUPER SMALL. And so we did. I bought my dress at JC Penney's, on sale for $200, and loved it. It was slender throughout which made me look like a mermaid, had beautiful off the shoulder straps, and it even had a small train in the back – perfect! We got married on a rainy night in January, in a small and lovely stain-glassed chapel. We only invited our immediate families, we all dressed up in formal wear, my dad gave me away, and Greg's dad married us. After Greg dipped me back dramatically for our "you may now kiss the bride" kiss, we strutted out of the chapel, both of us beaming hugely to the The Proclaimers' "500 Miles," a rockin' Scottish song that Greg often sang to me. It was the perfect wedding – with the bonus that we didn't go into debt getting married!

We had our honeymoon in Colorado, which Greg and I had often talked about visiting, and being there really got our juices flowing about maybe living there one day. And so, about nine months after we married, we moved to Denver! Neither of us had a concrete job, but we both soon found employment downtown. We lived in a loft that used to be an old warehouse, only owned one car, and walked everywhere or took the free "trolley" bus that ran up and down the main street. There was so much raw beauty there. We filled our free time with hiking in the foothills, hanging out at The Tattered Cover Bookstore (coolest independent bookstore ever), rollerblading or running along the creek paths, or taking scenic drives into little mountain towns. A couple years later we ended up moving back to Dallas for our careers, but Denver always held a special place in our hearts.

At another point in our lives, we tried to have kids. We got checked out and knew that my environment was hospitable and that Greg was not shooting blanks, but for some reason, nothing happened. And not for lack of effort. We decided if we could not get pregnant naturally, then we did not want to pursue it further with medical technology or adoption. I, myself, am adopted and totally advocate adoption – I think it's a wonderful thing; especially for me who totally lucked out with the best parents and siblings a girl could ask for. However, for Greg and I, it was too overwhelming to think of pursuing adoption or medical assistance to get pregnant. We knew either option would be a long road with many hurdles and would take a lot of patience, positive thinking and finances. Plus, Greg and I both were extremely happy with just each other. We knew we would love having a child if it happened for us, but if it didn't; well, we were already content with just "us." So when nothing happened, we were A-Okay with this (really).

Greg and I also have different thoughts and feelings about certain topics that are not mainstream; we don't fit into specific molds regarding politics or religion.

I guess what I'm trying to say is… we don't always go with the flow of society. We love living our lives the way we want to, on our own terms. It is incredibly refreshing, even though sometimes we tire of answering the tedious questions of people who don't get it and who want to argue with us about how we should live our lives.

But, moving to a foreign country? Quitting our successful careers with no plans to work? When we are just beginning our 4th decade of life? That seemed "out there," even for us!

Here we were considering moving to a foreign country, but Greg and I had never even traveled that much. I actually happened to possess a passport, but I had only been out the country a few times: to Paris with my mom (which turned out to be an incredible girls' trip), and a few times to Mexico with Greg at all-inclusive resorts. Although, I am not even sure Mexico can be considered a "foreign country" for those of us who live in Texas.

I am not a travel-bug type of person, but my husband is (ironically I had a passport, and he did not). He's always talking about wanting to go places, most of them out of the country; this goes back to that "dreamer" thing. It is one of those differences between us. You spend a huge chunk of money and then it's gone. Yes, you have the memories and pictures, but you can also have cool memories (and pictures) of things that happen in the States without having to travel very far. In fact, we could just stay in Dallas.

I had so many questions to answer. Did I want to move far away from Dallas? Did I want to leave the job where I had been for 18 years? Did I want to leave my friends and family? Did we have enough money to do this?

So, I thought. And I contemplated. And I considered.

And the more I thought things over... .

Heck, yes I could leave Dallas! The summers are miserably hot, and the winters don't last long enough. Even though the winter climate is mild, there always seem to be a few ice storms. One time I was sure I was going to crash and burn while sliding my way home after work in my little chili-red Mini Cooper S.

There are huge cockroaches in Dallas, a dreadful repulsion of mine. (I later found out there are cockroaches in Costa Rica as well. Who knew?)

I do have a few good friends in Dallas, but we didn't see each other that often, except for those I worked with. I knew I could keep in touch with them if I moved away, and I could see them when I visited, just as I do with friends in my home state of Wisconsin and in other parts of the country.

Greg's folks had always been super cool with giving us our space, and letting us visit when we wanted, and I didn't feel bad about moving away from them as long as Greg was okay with it. I have always been close with his parents, and I knew they would be happy for us and want us to do what we wanted to do. My own family had put up with my living several states away for a long time, so I figured Greg's family could give us up, as well.

Since we talked every other day and even visited one another at least a couple of times each year, I hoped my relocation would not upset my mom. With the technology of FaceTime and Skype, we could talk and see each other every day if we wanted. And since my mom was already a world traveler, I knew she would come visit us frequently.

Did we have enough money? Well, despite our large house and cars and toys, we had always budgeted and saved money. We knew that if we were serious about this, we had some time before we moved to put away additional money. Cost of living seemed as if it could be more affordable for us in Costa Rica, particularly if we ate local foods, rented frugally, and watched our money closely. Besides, I do love a good challenge.

There was something else I couldn't get out of my mind.

My Dad had died when I was 31 years old. It was way too soon, and it really knocked me off my feet. If you had known my dad, you would have seen him as, well, everything good. He was smart, quiet, loving, strong, honest, athletic, introspective, handsome – and he could do anything… seriously! What? You need a well drilled for your new house? No problem. You need some blueprints drawn up? No problem. You want to shoot some hoops? No problem (and he would let you win, even though he could beat you hands down). You need a complete house built? No problem. You want a beautiful piece of handmade wooden furniture? No problem. You need advice on business or a relationship or friendship? No problem (and he would always be right). You need guidance on the error of your ways? No problem (he would be disappointed, but surprisingly understanding and empathetic).

I could go on and on, but you get the gist. He died of cancer at 59. He had taken early retirement the year before, but couldn't enjoy it very much. He was recovering from his first round of cancer treatments, with the threat hanging over him that it could come back. And it did. It breaks my heart that, after all the hard work he put into his job over his entire adult life to support our family of six, he never got to retire and have fun doing non-work stuff. I wish he was here so we could talk this over, but he left me with the gift of knowing him pretty well. I can guess at his questions and his thoughts with what I believe to be a fair amount of accuracy. I think he would be proud of my adventurousness.

Greg's dad had been in poor health for a long time, but amazingly was still working, albeit part time. We knew his days were numbered. He had diabetes, which affected both his feet so that he couldn't walk and had to rely on a power chair to get around. Already he had suffered several heart attacks, and then, kidney failure, which required dialysis. He had been in and out of the hospital in the past few years, but he seemed to bounce back each time, and kept trucking along.

At the same time, we had a cousin's husband pass away in his early 40's, leaving his wife a widow and a newborn son fatherless. He had seemed relatively healthy; it was a fluke of pneumonia that landed him in the hospital, then a series of other things went wrong. Then, before we knew it, he was gone.

Who knows how long we have to live? I could be hit by a bus (Costa Rican or otherwise) tomorrow. There was no reason not to do something "crazy" – or at least give it a 100 percent effort. How could we regret it? We could always move back.

Maybe this dream *could* become a reality.

5. where to land

We researched Panama and Ecuador briefly, but quickly ruled them out. Ecuador was pretty far away and seemed to have higher incidents of crime and kidnapping. Panama seemed to have fewer places we would want to live, and also too warm of a climate for us.

The winner seemed to be Costa Rica. It kept popping up as having everything we would desire:

* It didn't seem too far away from the States (i.e., it is a four-hour airplane trip from Dallas).

* Costa Ricans were known to be welcoming and friendly to people from the United States (a foreign experience in a foreign country!).

* The country's government is stable and peaceful, there has been no military since 1948 (I now have a T-shirt that says this!).

* There is good, affordable health care and easy Internet access and Wi-Fi throughout the country.

* They speak Spanish, which we had wanted to learn for some time. (Greg and I both took German

in high school, don't ask me why Greg chose German over Spanish when he lived in Texas.)

* You can find reasonably priced houses to rent, fully furnished.

* Crime seemed to be relegated to petty theft, unlike the drug cartels and kidnappings that plague some other Latin American countries.

Of course, being who I am, I was skeptical and conservative and overly cautious. I felt like I sometimes needed to anchor my dreamer husband, and so, all in light of doing my "job", I set out to do my own research.

What did I find? Well, things such as this:

* "Suicide showers" are the norm, meaning hot water on demand via exposed electrical wires running straight to the shower head (I kid you not!).

* Heavily pot-holed roads, roads that are completely washed away, and awfully aggressive drivers. There are usually no street signs, and stop signs are not heeded by anyone – they are thought of as "suggestions" more than anything.

* Pedestrians do not have the right of way.

* The steak and beef do not taste as good as they do in the States (the cows are grass-fed only, which makes the steak less tender).

* There are many power outages.

* There can also be water outages.

* Earthquakes! (I had never been through an earthquake before.)

* Everything appears to take forever to accomplish, and I was used to getting stuff done fast (the Costa Ricans actually have a word for this: *tico time*).

* And last but certainly not least: B U G S!!! Scorpions, snakes, roaches, and spiders of a size you have never seen before (read: TARANTULAS)! You can imagine how I liked reading this last part, being a self-diagnosed arachnophobe... . Great.

Well, that settled it. How was I going to break this news to Greg? There was no way I could do this. ABSOLUTELY NO WAY. I mean, I have a problem with cockroaches as it is; we were paying good money to have the best pest control service spray our house every three months for the sole purpose of preventing me from having to see a cockroach – ever! And it worked: I hadn't seen one in my house in a very long time.

My husband is the King of Laid Back. He has always been easy-going, and of course that is also why he's so great for me.

So I told him my newfound information about bugs and spiders in Costa Rica, and how there was NO WAY I could entertain the thought of moving there. He was very calm and collected.

"Babe, it's cool. I read about that, too, but I'll always be there to protect you and kill bugs and spiders for you. Plus, there are lots of places in the Central Valley that are higher in elevation, and the bugs don't hang out up there; it's too cold for them at night."

"Really?" I responded. "There are places we can live where I'll never see a bug?"

"Well, I wouldn't say 'never', but there's the distinct possibility that you won't see too many bugs. And most likely not any snakes; they don't like it where it is colder because they are cold-blooded. But hey, you don't have to make up your mind just now. Let's take our time and think about it."

"Okay," (but still thinking, NO WAY!).

Then I had a brilliant idea. I opened my laptop and Google-searched for mosquito canopy netting. If they could keep mosquitoes out, they had to keep scorpions, spiders, roaches and snakes out, too, right? I was already envisioning myself cocooned in a beautiful white canopy that draped elegantly over my bed from a hoop in the ceiling. Romantic scenes from "The Thomas Crown Affair" were circling through my head.

Maybe, just maybe, I could sleep at night.

6. money, money, money

Well, let's be frank. We can't just quit our jobs in our early 40's, move to a foreign country, and live on *nothing!*

I had serious concerns about our having enough money, as we were not going to touch our 401K's for another 15-18 years. We were determined not to do that.

With Greg and I researching together, we quickly ascertained that if we lived in Costa Rica, we would either have to:

> * leave the country every 90 days, and have the expense of traveling to a bordering country or back to the U.S.;
>
> OR
>
> * apply for residency, which would enable us to avoid having to leave the country every 90 days.

Unlike most expats (*expat* is short for *expatriate*, meaning someone who lives outside of their native country) who are of retirement age and apply for "pensionado" residency, we were too young to have social security or monthly pensions. Therefore, we would have to apply for "rentista" residency, which would require us to prove that we had a certain amount of money for the first two years, and then a subsequent amount for the third and fourth years. At year three, we would be able to apply for "permanente" residency, which would eliminate the requirement for a monthly income.

The amount for the first two years is deposited into a CD, and once a month for 24 months, an amount from this CD is converted from dollars into colones for us to use for monthly expenses. If we do not need this entire monthly amount, we are able to reinvest it.

What about cost of living? From our research, and according to Facebook friends I had found in Costa Rica, most of whom were extremely helpful, you could rent a fully furnished house fairly inexpensively. If we looked, we might even find a deal for $400-600 for a two-bedroom, two-bath furnished house. This was unheard of in Dallas!

All my new expat friends on Facebook told me to rent, not buy. They said that many gringos (*gringo* is a term for foreigners, or really anyone other than a *tico* which is what a Costa Rican calls himself) come into Costa Rica with big dreams and plans, buy some property, and build their house. To me, that is just too much work, and you are just asking for trouble if you are not able to speak the language.

If, and when, the homeowners want to sell the house, it is a no go. In other words, it is very easy to buy, but not so easy to sell. Come to think of it, maybe that is why the inexpensive furnished houses to rent were so plentiful!

We did not want to be in that situation of not being able to sell, so if we decided to move to Costa Rica, we determined up front that we would be renting. Plus, renting would enable us to move around the country and experience different cities if we wanted.

If we could change our lifestyle a bit and buy only locally produced food, we would save money and be a lot healthier. A win/win! Costa Rica is known for its amazing farmers' markets where the fruits and vegetables are plentiful and inexpensive. That sounded great to us; we were so ready for a healthy change!

One day, while I was crunching numbers in an Excel spreadsheet, Greg walked in, interrupted me and said, "Babe, I think we need to go there for a visit. The money might or might not come together, but we are due for a vacation anyway, so let's go check it out, see if we like it there, and if it's even plausible for us to move there."

Indeed. We *were* due a vacation. This seemed like the perfect opportunity to get away and enjoy ourselves, and at the same time, to practice some "due diligence" (as the expats call on-the-ground research).

I closed my laptop and replied spontaneously, "How soon can we go?"

PART II – EXPLORING THE DREAM

7. trip time

Surprising to some people was the fact that my mom was going to come with us on our due diligence trip to Costa Rica. My mom is a pretty cool, down-to-earth chick. After raising four kids and dealing with all of our issues, nothing really surprises her anymore. She is a cute and petite little thing of a woman and certainly does not look her age (no numbers will be mentioned). She sometimes (still) seems to have more energy than me! She goes to a workout class several times a week called "Silver Sneakers" and always eats healthy. She keeps extremely busy; I can barely keep up with her schedule. Besides traveling around the world (Hong Kong, Italy and France, to name a few), she also has several girlfriends in her town that keep her going – either having lunch, volunteering together, or playing bridge. She is also part of a group called "The Juliets" – they are the cutest bunch of happy ladies, despite all of them having lost their husbands at some point. They regularly meet for breakfast once a week and sometimes do short trips together. Once, they even let me crash their breakfast party and I had so much fun meeting them all!

I was a little nervous about first telling our news to Mom. When the time arrived, I asked her to sit down, which helped. It also helped that she had known we were researching alternatives to Greg's job. So, when I told her that we wanted to visit Costa Rica as a possible place to retire early, she was very calm and collected. She had lots of questions, and we talked at length about it. She was cautiously excited for us. Then I told her we were going there for a trip and asked her if she wanted to come along. She said YES right away; she didn't even have to think about it, which is one of the many reasons why I love her. We told her it would be mostly "work" (due diligence) and not a lot of "play" – but she was totally up for the challenge.

Greg gets along really well with my mom, so we were both happy to have her come along. We knew that if we got too infatuated with Costa Rica, she would help pull us down to earth with her practical attitude.

We all spent time researching traveling in Costa Rica. My mom was concerned that we would need various shots before visiting a "third-world country," but surprisingly, none were required. Although many people think Costa Rica is a third-world country, it is more accurately known these days as a developing country. My mom even consulted with her doctors, but nope, no shots were needed – a huge sigh of relief on my part. If a trip to Costa Rica required shots, this whole Costa Rican adventure might have ended right here!

In early January 2012, the three of us, all tired of the bleak winter weather in the U.S., found ourselves onboard an international flight from Dallas to Costa Rica.

The four-hour flight was uneventful. I knew we were not going to Mexico, but it really began to seem as if Costa Rica was just around the corner.

Before we touched down, we began to see beautiful blue skies and gorgeous mountains and valleys out our window, and my photographer hubby began snapping pictures. We arrived at the airport and sailed through customs with no problems.

We exited the airport through swarms of people who were shouting and offering their taxi/driver services. We tried not to look bewildered while searching for a "big, white, bald-headed man." Needless to say, there were not many "big, white, bald-headed men" in the exit area, and Danny, the owner of the bed-and-breakfast where we would be staying in Grecia, was easily found.

Here is a little something not everyone knows about me: I am a meticulous, over–the-top planner and organizer of all things. That means that when Greg and I go on a trip, I have to plan everything (and I do mean everything). I cannot trust Greg to help me. The one time I did, we ended up on a "surprise" trip from

Dallas to Denver for a week with no credit cards and no way of paying for anything. To his credit, however, he was only thinking of me and trying to romantically surprise me. I let him off the hook because we had only been married a few months at the time, so he wasn't fully trained yet.

I had spent hours online researching different things for our trip: cities that we might want to check out, how we would travel in the country, where we would stay, where we would eat, what credit or debit cards we could use, and where we could withdraw cash (or colones, the local currency).

Grecia, which means "Greece" in Spanish, has a population of approximately 16,000 people, and is the capital city of the canton which shares the name "Grecia," in the province of Alajuela, Costa Rica. We had read that Grecia is a small, quaint, non-touristy town. Just a short 45-minute drive from the airport, it sounded like the perfect place to glimpse how the locals live.

Sometimes my planning and organizing pays off, as it did with the little place I found in Grecia. It was a small, modest B&B right in the heart of the town. We could easily walk around and find our way back each night. Danny, the owner, was very responsive to my emails (super organized people tend to have a lot of questions) and quite helpful. I was a little concerned that he didn't want a credit card deposit to hold our reservation: "Just pay me in American cash when you get here, no worries." Hmm, cash? Okay... .

We all liked Danny immediately; he was indeed big, white and bald. He spoke in Spanish to the parking attendant and then confidently maneuvered our way out of the airport into scary and aggressive-looking traffic. He is from Canada and had a totally laid-back, carefree demeanor about him. With a big ole happy grin on his face and his easy way of chatting with anyone, we felt comfortable with him right away.

On the drive to Grecia, Danny talked and answered our many questions:

Did he like living in Grecia? (Yes, very much.)

What was the climate like? (Temps rarely got above 85, and settled into the high 50's-60's at night or in the rainy season.)

What kind of prices could you rent a house for here? (Anywhere from $300 and higher, depending on what you wanted.)

What kind of computer did he recommend? (Anything Apple.)

How was the Wi-Fi? (Great, actually throughout the country Wi-Fi was plentiful.)

Could we use our iPhones here? (Yes, in fact he had an iPhone! We would just need to change something out called a "SIM card" to have a Costa Rican number.)

Could we get mail here somehow? (Yes, there is a post office that had P.O. boxes you could rent.)

How did he pay his bills? (At the grocery store.)

The 45-minute trip went by very quickly with all my questioning and Danny's answering. It was a little warm out, but with the windows rolled down (notice I said "rolled") there was a nice breeze, and we enjoyed our drive and visit with Danny as we cruised down the highway toward Grecia.

We had arrived!

8. darn good coffee and old time gas stations

It is said that Grecia is the "used car capital" of Costa Rica, and as we exited from the Pan American Highway (which is nothing special, just a one-lane, sometimes two-lane highway, but one of the nicer roads in Costa Rica), we began to see one car dealership after another. Mind you, these are not like car dealerships in North America; they are small operations, and they sell mostly used cars.

We arrived at the B&B, and Danny took our bags to our rooms and then gave us a tour of the inn. When Danny had previously described it as "modest," he wasn't kidding, but everything was very clean and neat. The kitchen was available for us to use, and just past the kitchen was a lovely, shaded, outside courtyard with comfy chairs where we could sit and watch the birds come and go. There was even a big water cooler in the kitchen, even though Danny said it was fine to drink out of the tap. I was happy to hear what my research had indicated; this was not Mexico – throughout Costa Rica, it is fine to drink water straight from the faucet!

Something I was not prepared for were the barbed wire and gates surrounding most of the houses in central

Grecia. When we arrived at the B&B, Danny had to open his front gate, which had coils of barbed wire on top, and somehow maneuvered his car into the tiny "porch" area in the front of the house.

I looked over at Mom and saw her eyeing all the barbed wire and heavy sliding gates and knew she was pretty worried. I mean, barbed wire just doesn't give you warm, fuzzy feelings. But Mom is good about keeping an open mind, and I tried to do the same.

It turns out that barbed wire, bars on windows, and fences completely surrounding houses are all very traditional in Spanish and Latino cultures. You may recall early paintings of medieval Spain where a pretty señorita is hiding behind a fan and peering out her balcony window at a guitar-strumming caballero serenading her from below. If you look closely, her window has bars on it. Yes, they were for security, but just as important, they were to keep those caballeros from being able to get to those señoritas! The bars are as much about tradition and culture as they are about security.

We cleaned up and relaxed a bit and then headed out for dinner. We walked a few blocks to "one of the best steakhouses" around, the Galería (note: the Galería has since closed and is no longer there). We were famished, and this place did not disappoint! Even though the steak tastes different here in Costa Rica, it was very good at the Galería, and the service was phenomenal.

I was proud to use some Spanish right away, and our waitress was amazing. As soon as she saw us trying to speak as much Spanish as we could, she became very kind and helpful (and she knew a good bit of English even though she claimed to know "just a little").

After dinner I ordered *café con leche* (coffee with milk), and it was superb! The coffee was rich and strong, with steamed milk mixed into the coffee, so it was almost like a latte. I took a sip, and sighed. It was quite simply the best "coffee with milk" I had ever experienced.

Away I went to La-La Land, dreaming of Greg bringing this coffee to me in bed every morning, and I began to think that perhaps the coffee alone might be a good enough reason to move here!

The next day, Danny told us about a group of expats that were going to meet that morning at a little café for breakfast, and he said, "If you want, I can call one of them to make sure they're meeting, and let them know to expect you. They are all really nice, and I know they would be happy to chat with you and answer any questions."

So, off we went to Café Electa, and low and behold, there was a whole group of gringos there. They greeted us warmly. The expats were easy to talk to and very welcoming. We had several great cups of coffee with them.

This time, again, I ordered my *café con leche* (usually I drink coffee black, but after the experience of the previous night...). They brought out a cup and saucer, poured some very steamy black coffee into my cup, and then set a small pitcher down beside it. I whispered to Greg, "Okay, that's nice that they gave me extra coffee, but where is the milk?"

Upon looking in the pitcher, I saw it *was* my milk, all steamy and hot! Wow! So cool! (Hot, actually.) What a professional touch, to give you hot steamed milk to put in your hot coffee, rather than cold milk, which doesn't really make sense. Why would you want to cool down your hot cup of coffee?

I soon found out that this is how coffee and milk are served in many places in Costa Rica. Being a coffee lover, and after having two awesome coffee experiences in my first two days, I knew I was falling in love – at least with the *coffee* in Costa Rica. How bad could it possibly be to live where there was such great coffee?

One of the gringos at breakfast was a gentleman who had been here for many years and was married to a tica. We talked to him about our trip, that we were here for the first time and were trying to decide if moving here was the right thing for us. He soon told us he was a realtor who dealt with both sales and rentals, and if we weren't doing anything after breakfast, "I could take you for a drive and show you some rentals and how much they go for, just to give you an idea."

Well, shoot, that sounded awesome! We were starting to see already how truly kind people were in Costa Rica. We offered to pay for some gas, which was the only thing he would accept, and away we went to the gas station.

As we pulled into the gas station, I suddenly had a sense of déjà vu: being a child and pulling into a full-service gas station in the early 70's with my parents. We sat inside the car, while the service people ran around and filled up the gas, cleaned the windshield, and asked our new friend what else he wanted. We soon found out that all gas stations here are full service; in fact – you are not allowed to pump your own gas, even if you want to. It was like a step back in time.

We told the realtor that we thought we would prefer the views and the climate of the higher elevation on the ridges, so he drove up into the hills above Grecia and showed us different areas and rental houses.

At one point, we stopped to visit one of his friends who had tons of plants next to his house. The beautiful plants were in a covered arboretum, and we had a friendly chat while he led us down the different rows of his garden and told us about all his different herbs and plants. I began to envision a huge front porch with potted herbs scattered haphazardly. I could pick from them at my leisure and create gourmet meals for Greg and me. How fun!

In the middle of our discussion about rosemary and basil, the realtor saw another friend of his across the street and pulled us away from our plant discussion. He asked if she would mind chatting with us, and she said, "Sure, come on over!" People were so friendly here! She welcomed us into her house, which was a simple but spacious 2-bedroom with a beautiful back yard. She had just finished painting the rooms in different vibrant colors. This lady was amazing. As she talked to us, she told us of all the different places she had lived around the world, and how she was now living in Costa Rica by herself. She was currently taking a painting class – ALL in Spanish, even though she was not fluent. Wow. I had admiration overload for her. Now I could see myself painting or doing crafts of some kind. I had previously painted step

stools for children with their names in calligraphy –
which were a huge hit. Who's to say I couldn't do that
again, or take up watercolor painting or some other
kind of craft? If we moved here, I would have time,
time to do ANYTHING I wanted. The options were
starting to spin non-stop in my head… .

Most of the places the realtor was pointing out to us
for rent were fully furnished. He showed us one large,
attractive house with a big fenced-in backyard and
mature fruit trees everywhere, renting for $800 a
month.

Greg looked at me and said, "Man, that house would
be so cool! We could walk out to our trees in the
morning and pick our own fruit for breakfast! Just
think about it. How great would that be?"

He had a good point. I imagined Greg picking and
bringing me fruit while I blended us up smoothies, and
then we would drink them while sitting in huge
rocking chairs on our porch, watching the sun come
up.

Wow. This could really be the life!

9. the beach

During our research, we had learned that Costa Ricans drive very aggressively. Having much less experience behind the wheel than their North American counterparts, combined with a machismo world view, seems to create in them a uniquely non-defensive, yet ultra-aggressive driver.

We were about to get our first taste of this. We were driving a rental car to our next destination: Playa Hermosa in the province of Guanacaste, which is on the west coast of Costa Rica. You cannot go to Guanacaste and *not* see a beach; they are everywhere along the endlessly long coast, mostly small beaches, one after the other. A lot of times while in the U.S., you might think, "Oh, I'm driving to that city over there, which is 20 miles away; it should take me about 20 minutes." But in Costa Rica, it actually takes you 45 minutes to drive 20 miles for a variety of reasons: the roads frequently are not paved well; there is a lot of traffic; there is only one lane most of the time; and there are rivers with one-way bridges to cross (where you have to wait until there is no one coming, and then make a run for it).

We weren't really sure how long this drive would take us – anywhere from four to eight hours, most of it on the Pan American Highway. We had rented a fairly new Nissan SUV, so at least we felt okay if we happened to encounter any small rivers without bridges that we needed to cross. I was nervous for Greg to drive, but he assured me he was up to the task.

He did great, I must say. And the drive was pretty much uneventful – at least for Mom and me. However, by the time we got there, seven hours later, I could hear Greg audibly breathe a sigh of relief. He peeled his white-knuckled hands off the steering wheel and pronounced, "Okay, who's ready for a beer?"

Our hotel was *right* on the "Playa Hermosa" beach, with a perfect view of the ocean from the outdoor café connected to it. We ordered some drinks, relaxed and soaked it all in. There were colorful birds flying around and landing nearby. A few people casually strolled along the beach, and I liked that this didn't seem to be a tourist place, just a small, cozy, local beach. It was pretty warm and muggy, but with a slight breeze and our cool drinks, we happily toasted "*pura vida*" to each other and clinked our glasses.

"Pura vida" is an expression used often here. It means a bit of everything: "take it easy, life is good, go with the flow, it is what it is." Literally translated, it means "pure life."

After our drinks we decided to take a stroll along the beach. It was lovely out! We took off our shoes and carried them, Mom rolled up her pants, and we took a long walk enjoying the sights and sounds of the ocean.

Suddenly we heard several loud squawking sounds in symphony. We looked up and Greg pointed out that those bright green things were parrots! They were flying high above us – landing briefly on the tops of palm trees, then taking off again. It was amazing to see them; it was the first time for me seeing them in the "wild"!

We were taking our time, walking along the beach with the waves lapping our legs, all of us looking up at the parrots, when all of a sudden – SPLASH! Mom was down. One second she was walking beside me, the next she was on her butt sitting on the ocean floor – arms flailing around and exclaiming "OHHHH!"

Her purse was taken down with her as well. Poor thing. I guess a more ferocious than usual wave took her by surprise while she was looking the other way. We helped her up right away, but she was loaded down with surf and sand and thoroughly soaked. I guess that's one way to cool off. We headed back to the hotel for her to rinse off and change.

Later, we had dinner at a lovely, quaint restaurant on the beach. We each ordered the *casado*. A "casado" is a typical Costa Rican meal with your choice of meat (beef or chicken, sometimes fish), rice, beans, plantains and avocado, and sometimes an egg. It was very tasty and filling. What is not to love about the peaceful sound of ocean waves crashing in while you eat a yummy meal with good company, and a perfect sunset to top it off?

I did notice some fellow tourists dining around us, but it still seemed more of a local beach, where Costa Ricans and expats hang out and jog up and down the shoreline. I don't know when I had started liking non-touristy areas because when we went to Mexico for vacations, we chose the nicest all-inclusive resorts we could find and they were 100-percent touristy! Maybe I was beginning to think of Costa Rica as a home and not as a vacation destination.

Greg had told me before we came that I could take my time with making a decision. He would never pressure me into something I didn't want to do, no matter how right it was for him. Of course, there was no question of *his* decision. I had told him I wanted to take in the whole trip, relax and think about things before making my final decision.

My mom knew all this, too, which didn't help, because every couple hours when we would experience something new (good or bad), she would ask me if I was making any "headway on my decision." I was always noncommittal and replied with, "Uh… I don't know" or "Hmmmm, I'm not sure yet."

They probably thought I was trying to be mysterious or something, but I really didn't know yet which way I was leaning, and I certainly didn't want to be pressured into leaning in a particular direction. I knew my husband desperately needed this, but there *were* other options for him, and I had to feel right about it for myself or I wouldn't be happy. This was *not* a decision I was looking forward to making. I was actually trying not to stress out about it.

For two days we toured several beach areas, visiting Playa Flamingo, Playa Tamarindo (a popular surfing beach), Playa Ocotal, and Playa Hermosa. We visited several different grocery stores – from a spacious, modern American-style one (*pricey!*) – to a small, local, tico-style one (*affordable!*). It was odd to see liquor, along with the beer and wine, in all the grocery stores; this is against the law in Texas. We also visited a vet and a family doctor (both of whom looked about 16 years old and spoke flawless English) – it was good to learn that there were competent doctors to take care of our personal needs and those of our dog.

We also met with a realtor who showed us around for some comparison-shopping on house rentals. We actually saw one place, a three-story modern condo, all glass and beautiful staircases and balconies, approximately 3,000 square feet, and when you walked out the back door and through a little gate, BAM – there was the ocean! And, not more than 20 yards from the gate, your own perfect, private beach! Rent: $1,000 per month. What? Crazy!

It seemed to be true what we had heard: people build houses all over Costa Rica, and then, when they want to move, they can't sell them. They end up renting them (usually furnished) just to have someone in the house and paying the mortgage. What a steal!

We truly loved the beach, but in the end, we just couldn't see living in the hot, humid climate every day. It felt just like Dallas in the summer, but it would be year-round. Especially on our budget, the huge air-conditioning bills could kill us, and there is no way we could live without AC on the beach in Costa Rica!

If we were to move here (which was still a big "if" at this point), we knew we at least wanted to start out in a cooler climate. The beach could always happen later.

10. the volcano

Our next destination was La Fortuna where there was supposed to be an active volcano. To get there, we had to drive around the north side of this HUGE lake – Lake Arenal. Greg put on his driving hat again and away we went. Just because the lake was huge, did not mean the road around it was huge. The road was narrow, with many blind curves and several one-way bridges, where we had to compete with on-coming cars for the opportunity to cross to the other side. Sometimes the GPS would just go out completely... . The curvy narrow road seemed to go on forever.

On top of all that, the directions we had from the spa/resort were kind of crazy. They read:

"From the Catholic church in La Fortuna, we are located 6 km west to the Arenal volcano."

Say what? Where is the address? We soon learned there ***are no addresses*** in Costa Rica! At least not in the "North American house number + Street name" sense. Here, the address is derived from distance to a landmark and sometimes that landmark no longer exists! How strange, I know, but it is what it is. Pura vida. There is some kind of limited postal service, and there are certainly places you can rent a P.O. box, but the "addresses" here are truly without numbers. Another example:

"On main El Cajón road, 500 meters from the Los Angeles church, 5th house on the right with white paint."

All of a sudden I started thinking, "Oh! How will I get all my catalogues that come to me EVERY SINGLE DAY?" Seriously – I get like 10+ catalogues a day. And at Christmas time? I actually felt sorry for my mail man… I'd come home to find my mailbox just bursting at the seams and overflowing. Victoria's Secret, Athleta, Title Nine, JCrew, Sierra Trading Post, Lands End, etc. (and if you're curious, Victoria's Secret totally wins by volume; they must have a mammoth printing press because they pump out catalogues every couple of days, and gentlemen, they have SO MUCH MORE than just bras and panties!).

Honestly, I kind of LOVE browsing through all my catalogues in depth, turning down page corners to mark my favorites, going online and looking at reviews and more pictures (different angles make a difference!) and then finally – ordering! Then, oh, the anticipation of delivery! The rushing to open and trying it on. And when it fits? And makes me look skinny? Totally a keeper! Joy! Happiness!! (Okay, I may have a slight problem.)

But, wait a second, if I don't have an address in Costa Rica… how…?? Oh. No.

Realization slowly hit me, that if I don't even have an address, *how* would I:

1. Receive catalogues, and

2. Order online to be delivered right to my door?

Could I live without my daily catalogue entertainment? This was honestly too traumatic to even think about.

But I get carried away… let's get back to the volcano. The whole reason we wanted to go to Arenal Volcano was because I had read about it erupting on a regular basis and we wanted to see the show. The Arenal area had made a killing on the volcano's regularity. People would stay at hotels and resorts in the area with rooms facing the volcano, in hopes of witnessing the eruption. We had heard the views at night were most spectacular – I imagined it to be like a huge lava lamp – gorgeous views of hot bright orange/red lava against a midnight black sky.

Shortly before we arrived, Danny from the B&B Grecia had told us that it was not erupting anymore – and hadn't for the past year and a half! Bummer. Oh well. We had reservations – so we were going regardless. Pura vida (see, this phrase is actually quite handy).

Lake Arenal and Arenal Volcano were both absolutely gorgeous. Even without the volcanic eruptions, and even though we had clouds hovering around the actual volcano peak the whole time we were there – it was still breathtaking. This was the only "touristy" part of our vacation as we had no due diligence work to do in Arenal, our only job was to relax and enjoy – and the spa/resort I had found was absolutely spectacular! Los Lagos was a little paradise – lizards climbed and birds and butterflies flew all around the tropical vegetation. The resort had several natural hot springs (heated by Arenal Volcano) which were relaxing and got hotter as you went higher up towards the volcano. The springs were all secluded in trees and plants – like being in a jungle with little lighted paths winding every which way. The pools had bars where you could swim up to order your drinks and the main dining area had no walls, so the tables looked out into the tropical vegetation and birds would come and perch right on the glassless window ledge.

With tiny umbrellas in our piña coladas, we forgot about making life-changing decisions for a while and just enjoyed being tourists.

11. the tarantula

Our Lake Arenal vacation had ended, and we made the drive back to Grecia with no problems – Greg was quickly becoming a great Costa Rican driver.

I was friends on Facebook with a guy from my small hometown in Wisconsin – we had not gone to high school together, nor did we know each other growing up. I had gone to the parochial high school, and he to the public one. But, as is sometimes the case with Facebook (and small towns), we had many mutual friends, and because of this we had easily connected through the power of social media.

He also just happened to live in Costa Rica with his family(!), and when he got wind of our upcoming trip to Costa Rica, invited us to his house for dinner one night. He lived in a suburb of San José called Escazú, which is about a 45-60 minute drive from Grecia where we were based. Danny at the B&B helped us hire a driver because we had heard that driving at night was not a good idea. Indeed, we had a traffic-filled drive in rush hour through the capital city and many windy roads up to my friend's house. We were happy to relax and have someone else do the driving.

My friend lived on the top of a mountain (seriously), and needless to say, it was an adventurous and treacherous drive! We found out later that our driver, Wilson of Coati Tours, had made the trip the *previous* day – just to scout it out and make sure he knew how to get us there. This was just another example of the tico-style hospitality (I mean, what kind of hired driver checks out the route ahead of time, just to make sure he doesn't have any glitches?).

I love the irony that the first time I met this guy was *not* in our small hometown, in which we both had lived for at least the first 18 years of our lives, but in Costa Rica – several (okay, many) years later!

We had a wonderfully good time – visiting people we'd never met before, but who graciously invited us into their home for a great evening of conversation, meeting their children, and enjoying a delicious gourmet meal. They were so friendly! We felt so welcome and were grateful for the opportunity to discuss our thoughts about moving to Costa Rica. They told us about the chickens they kept and how they had fresh eggs for breakfast every morning (Greg was very interested in this!). They had a beautiful home with spectacular views, and the highlight of the evening was after dark, when we could see the city lights for miles and miles. It was breathtaking.

Remember my self-diagnosis of arachnophobia? Well, it wasn't long before I got to see my first ever, live TARANTULA. It was not in a cage. We were not at a zoo. Did I mention that my mom does not like spiders EVEN MORE THAN ME? Parrots are the sort of thing you want to see in the wild, but a tarantula? No thank you.

After visiting our friends late into the night, we walked out the front door, and there – lo and behold – was Mr. Tarantula. Just hanging out in all his glory. He was motionlessly sprawled out on a huge column on the patio right outside their front door. At eye level.

He was HUGE! My mom couldn't even go near it (okay, me neither). Greg, of course, was super excited and trying to snap some pictures, totally enthralled.

Our friends, who I think were secretly laughing at Mom and me, just said "Oh, that little thing? What's the big deal?"

My friend's wife even ventured to say, "Oh, I kill spiders all the time. You know they're *really* big when you hear them go THUMP when they hit the floor."

OH. MY. GOD.

12. the last dinner

For our last night in Costa Rica, we stayed at the B&B in Grecia and celebrated with dinner again at the Galería – I was craving that excellent coffee.

The weather was perfect and we had a lovely, peaceful three-hour meal sitting on their back outdoor patio. Actually, we asked for the bill two hours into dinner, but... you know, tico-time, we didn't get it for another hour – which was fine with us. They just took their time bringing *la cuenta* (the bill) to us. Much later I was to discover that the bill is *not* normally brought to the table after dining, but rather, you are to get up and go to the bar or cashier to pay when finished. They will gladly bring the bill to the table if you ask for it, but this is not the standard procedure.

As it was our last night, we had a lot to talk about: Costa Rica, Greg and I possibly moving there, the uncertainty of a major change, the tarantulas(!), etc. And the final verdict was – why don't we take some more time to think about it before making any decisions? (And when I say "we", I mean me.)

The next day we enjoyed a leisurely breakfast made by our excellent B&B hosts – which always included bananas, pineapple and mango (so good!). We packed, and made our way to the airport. Thanks to Danny, we knew that before we checked in for our flight, we needed to go to a certain area right inside the front airport door to pay an "exit fee" of $28 per person. Yep, we had to *pay* before exiting Costa Rica and returning to the United States – kind of odd. Or maybe they do this in all foreign countries. I had no idea; I am *so* not a world traveler. And yet here I am, considering moving to Costa Rica... .

We splurged on lunch at Schlotzsky's in the airport, and paid a huge amount of money for it. But it was yummy, hit the spot, and we were still on vacation. Right?

Our flight had a stop in Houston first, before going to Dallas. We didn't know before hand, but of course it made sense that we would go through customs at the first place we landed in the States. This was not fun. There were lines and lines of people, both at customs and immigration. And, yep, we had a flight to catch for Dallas that was upon us before we knew it. We were stressing out about making our connecting flight. Luckily some agent finally took pity on us and told us, "Just leave your luggage here, and RUN! Trust us, we'll take care of it!"

What else could we do? We left our luggage where he pointed, hoped for the best, and ran to our connecting gate. We JUST BARELY made it onto our flight.

We got back to Dallas fine. But guess what? Our luggage did not. Luckily they found out where our luggage was and said they would deliver it to our door later that night – mainly because Mom was scheduled to fly out the next day to Wisconsin, so she absolutely needed hers.

At 3:00 in the morning there was a knock on our door, and there they were – with all of our luggage. Later that morning, I dropped Mom off at the Dallas Fort Worth airport, with constant promises that I'd keep her posted about my decision-making progress.

And suddenly – our Costa Rican due diligence trip had officially ended.

That night, Greg and I found ourselves at home, trying to psych each other up to go back to work the next morning. I must admit, at that moment, the thought of quitting my job was never more appealing.

PART III – BEGINNING THE DREAM

13. decision time

My husband is the most patient person I know. He knew I needed time to think about all the pros and cons. I mean – this was a HUGE decision. But I also knew how he felt and what he wanted to do – quit our jobs, drop everything, and make this monumental life-changing move. After returning to Dallas, he didn't pester me, or even bring it up at all. Of course we talked about Costa Rica quite a bit, but he was careful never to say "when" we move there. It was always "if" we decide to move there. Which was very sweet of him.

After a few days of this, I told him that I would give myself two months to make my final decision. He told me, "No pressure at all, babe. You can take as long as you want. I want you to WANT to move there, IF that's what we decide, together. I don't want you to do this just for me. We have to be in this together. It's all for one, and one for all. I would be nowhere without you, and if we choose to stay here, we'll find another way around my work situation. We'll make it work."

See what I mean? I know. I have the most wonderful husband ever. But, I was emphatic that I *would* make my decision, one way or the other, in two months time.

A few nights later, I found myself alone for the evening and figured it was as good a time as any to do some soul-searching. I poured myself a glass of wine, got out a notebook and pen, turned on some George Winston and lit some candles. I looked at the calendar and saw that two months out came to mid-March. I was not looking forward to making this decision. I honestly didn't know what I wanted to do. I started with the most basic thing I knew – a pro and con list (a "Jen favorite" I picked up from my dad). Here are a few of the items I jotted down:

PROS:

Simplify our lives (material things, brand names, spending money, and even smaller things like how I dress, do my hair and makeup)

Live healthier

Time to do what we want

No more work stress, politics, problems

No temptations (like purchasing designer clothes/shoes/purses, or going out all the time – to eat/drink or concerts/symphony) – because we wouldn't have the income anymore, and also could replace these things with more natural, down to earth and less expensive things

Feel younger (?)

Spectacular views, nature

Time to develop businesses, blogs, hobbies

Enjoy life more (!)

Spend more time together

CONS:

Bugs (!!!!!)

Language barrier

Sahara (our dog) (?)

Grand piano (?)

Car (if get, expense, insurance, repairs, gas…)

Expense of either Residency or leaving country every 90 days

Get bored (?)

Miss being able to always get what we want (?)

Miss friends/family (?)

Miss concerts, going out to dinner (?)

Emotional – new culture, homesickness (?)

If I was perfectly honest with myself, my gut instinct was to stay where I was. I am a creature of habit. I *liked* my job. Sure it was tedious and stressful sometimes, but I was good at what I did, and I had been with my company (and some of the people who worked there) for almost 18 years. I was very content with my daily routine.

I loved our home. The neighborhood was gated and I felt secure jogging or walking early in the morning. There was a pond with trees and trails, kids played safely in the streets, traffic was light and slow, neighbors knew each other, and we had amazing friends who lived on either side of us. Our house was beautifully landscaped and decorated; our backyard wasn't huge, but it was cozy and had a shady patio. I REALLY LIKED everything about it.

I loved my Yamaha grand piano. This piano and I were MEANT to be together. I grew up playing piano and this was for sure the best piano I ever had. The tone and richness of the sound that came from it! I just loved playing it and felt one with it. Sure, I didn't play it all the time, but when I wanted to – I loved having it there, just beckoning to me.

I loved my chili-red Mini Cooper S. I know… it's just a car, but it was perfect for me too. It was cute, and sporty, and I loved zipping around in it.

I loved our dog, Sahara Lucy. We had rescued her after her first owner returned her to the breeder. We flew to Ohio to meet her, promptly fell in love, and drove back with her to Dallas and she was worth it. She is a huge American Mastiff, and a gentle 180-pound-giant whom I loved with all my heart. I wasn't sure, but it just seemed like it would be next to impossible to bring her to Costa Rica.

But now, here was the hard part: All these "favorite things" aside… were we really happy? We hardly ever had time to enjoy our material "toys," and more importantly, we hardly ever enjoyed (or saw) each other. When I thought about it – what good is a great house, neighborhood, cars, other things… if we were losing our happiness? Or our enthusiasm for life? Or our love for each other?

Don't get me wrong – Greg and I both knew we loved each other. But I believed we were both getting dragged into his work/stress cycle, and it was dragging our marriage down as well. And truly, I wasn't happy when my husband wasn't happy. We didn't have time to be happy with the black cloud of his job hanging over us. Greg's health was also rapidly deteriorating, and he was on high blood pressure medicine.

I guess this happens to couples all the time. One of the spouse's jobs gets unbearable, and there seems like no way out… and they just – stay – in the same pattern. And things get harder. I've seen it happen time and time again. Everyone wants more – more money, more house, more cars, better schools for their kids, etc. because of course, the harder the job gets, the more we try to make ourselves happy with splurging. But it doesn't always end with happily ever after. Too many marriages deteriorate because couples lose their perspective on what is really important.

Greg and I no longer allowed our jobs to define us. But with Greg's work ethic, and simply because he cared about doing a good job, his job would continue to overwhelm him until the day he quit (or retired).

It's true that you have to work at a marriage, and it's not always easy. I also knew that Greg was worth it to me. I knew he would do the same for me (actually, he would do MORE than the same for me; he would do anything for me). What did I have to lose? So what if we quit our jobs, and sold our house, got there and didn't like it? We could always move back, right? We could always get a job somewhere doing something.

Why not throw caution to the wind? Why not take a chance? Even if I took Greg's job out of the equation (because of course, he *could* get a different job doing something else) – we only have this one life – why *not* go on an adventure together? What was holding me back?

Just because I was scared of the unknown? Helen Keller or Amelia Earhart never got anywhere thinking like that, I'm sure of it. Maybe it was time to be brave and do something "unknown."

This whole Costa Rica thing originally may have been Greg's idea, but once I started thinking about it differently (to be fair, making it about ME), the whole "new life" suddenly started to appeal to me. Simplifying my life started making sense. I mean, why was I always spending so much money on clothes and going out for dinners and drinks? We spent SO much money doing these things!

What if these things (the designer jeans and hand bags, the huge house, the steakhouses and fine wine – things which, let's face it, weren't making us happy anyway) could be replaced by living a more simple life, and taking it easy, and spending more quality time together, exploring, doing what we wanted, and just being… HAPPY?

I suddenly realized that NOTHING was holding me back, and unexpectedly, I abruptly had my answer. Even though I knew there were hard decisions I would have to make (the dog, the piano), I knew without a doubt that I wanted to DO THIS, to take a chance, or at least to TRY IT.

Perhaps I was just feeling "wine brave" (did you think I was still on glass #1 after all this thinking?), but I felt assured I had made my decision. As long as we could satisfy my biggest concerns, I felt confident about my choice.

I was almost GIDDY to tell Greg, after all – he was resigned to waiting and being patient for two more months!

14. shhhhhhhhh

With the hardest part over, Greg and I spent a lot of time talking every night about details. Money, for one thing – I wanted to make sure we had enough to live on for some time without working (and without digging into our 401K's). I also wanted to be able to travel to the U.S. at least once a year to visit our families. It was hard to estimate accurately, as we didn't know exactly how much it would cost us to live there, except for the rent range. The food and utility bills would just have to be estimated. We weren't sure yet in what city we wanted to start – but we did agree that it would not be the beach, as it was too hot, but somewhere in the Central Valley instead.

We feared that if our employers found out what we were trying to do, they would fire us on the spot. Honestly – they probably would have just said, "Oh Okay, sure Jen-Jen – you're going to move to Costa Rica…," (head nodding, but all the while secretly thinking, "WHATEVER!!"). It seems really silly now, but at the time, we were worried about it, so our biggest hurdle was keeping our plans hush-hush as we went about selling stuff… our house, our furnishings, etc. We told people we were "downsizing," which was of course, the truth.

However, in today's society, "downsizing" is hard for people to comprehend because North Americans just move up, up, up – right? You can't own a lovely 2-story house in a beautiful gated community, and then (with no change in employment) move somewhere *smaller* and *cheaper*! It's like going from a Coach handbag to an old tattered backpack. I mean, who does that? (Oh wait – *I* actually ended up doing that!).

It was quite mind-opening for me, as people seemed confused and unaccepting of the simple fact that we wanted to downsize. If they thought we were crazy for doing that, just wait till they found out we were retiring early to Costa Rica! It was no one's business… but what if we just wanted to save more money? What if we had lots of debts we wanted to pay down? What if we wanted to get more value out of our money, like having a house that was comfortable but not way more than we needed? To me, that seems like a good thing, and not a bad idea at all – for people to pay off debts, save and invest money, and use their money more wisely. But the "American" way is to obtain more and more "things" while becoming more and more in debt. I totally empathize with people who wake up and decide to downsize no matter what anyone says; it's hard to do!

All of this made me *that* much more determined and assured that we were making the right decision. We were ready to do this!

So, we put our house up for sale almost immediately after making our decision, and then we waited.

And waited.

And waited.

And waited.

We didn't sell our house until 8 months later. Which was okay, for the most part, as we were able to take our time selling our furniture. We had a simple strategy for selling our furniture, appliances, jewelry and other household items. We put our best stuff up for auction on eBay, and if things didn't sell there, we tried Craigslist. From there, items were moved to our neighborhood online news group and a huge yard sale. Anything still remaining went to friends, family, and then finally – Goodwill.

By the time our house sold, we had successfully sold almost everything except for the items we still needed for day-to-day living.

The hardest thing for me to sell was not our house, but my piano – my lovely, shiny black Yamaha grand piano. I loved this piano! The tone was incredibly rich, and the way the keys mysteriously moved the way I wanted them to beneath my fingers was pure magic.

I am so thankful now for that day long ago when my parents heard about a neighbor who was selling their old-white-gawd-awful upright piano for $40. They bought it as a piece of furniture, painted it a couple coats of black, and stuck it in the corner of our bright-red family room (something needed to subdue all that red!).

One morning, I completely surprised my parents by playing a song on the piano. They had gone out the night before and the babysitter taught me a song by ear, which I picked up quickly and remembered. I played it again the next day. And every day after that. Over and over again. Probably drove my folks crazy. Their "piece of furniture" was suddenly something else entirely.

My folks soon started me on lessons with a very strict nun at my grade school – Sr. Malinda. Other students thought she was harsh, but I completely loved her. She taught me so much and was the perfect mixture of being hard on me but also encouraging with praise. I stayed with her through my grade school years and kept in touch with her for a very long time afterwards. I still have her pocket-size notebooks in which she wrote my lessons.

I kept on with my piano studies through high school, accompanying the Swing Choir as a freshman – which was intimidating, as you technically had to be a sophomore before trying out for Swing Choir. I remember my first day in the choir room, totally surrounded by UPPER classmen, and just wishing the grand piano would swallow me whole. Even though I was a totally-shy-nerdy-girl, a few of the popular senior class guys somehow took pity on me, and teased me in a sweet way, which made me feel more comfortable.

The summer after my junior year in high school, I tried out and somehow made it into a super cool musical touring group for the State of Wisconsin. It was an amazing group that every musician, vocalist and dancer in every high school in Wisconsin wanted to be in, called "The KIDS From Wisconsin." It was a group made up of about 32 people, and the auditions, held in Milwaukee, were highly competitive. I had a ragtime song I really liked playing (thank you Mr. Scott Joplin) and I guess they liked it too. I toured with them for two summers, and it truly was the most incredible time. We practiced, performed, lived and breathed next to each other all summer – so naturally, we all grew very close. I had my first "real" boyfriend that summer. I had my first true best-friend-forever girlfriend. We worked hard, but we played hard too. We performed live almost every single night for the whole summer. It was a summer of firsts for me – as I also had a solo(!) to perform – *every night.* I had NEVER liked performing solo, and it made me crazy to think about playing live, all by myself, in front of huge crowds of people. But the more I did it, the less nervous I became. The crowds were so energetic, and I even got some *"Standing O's"* (as we called them, short for "standing ovations"). I made some amazing and fantastic friends – some of whom I am still in touch with to this day, including that first real boyfriend and BFF.

I continued my piano studies in college – I minored in music and was awarded a small scholarship. I had the best professor there for my piano lessons – I loved Dr. Kohn! He was a very tall man, kind of gruff and stern with a booming voice, but he was also a completely sweet grandfatherly figure to me. He loved to sing and dance around me while I was playing for him in our lessons, which made me totally nervous, but that was just his way of encouraging me. Instead of filling my college days with drinking and partying, I spent my time practicing piano. I lived and breathed music, and I loved it! I accompanied whoever would pay me – vocalists, instrumentalists, choirs, opera theatre, etc.

The professor (who now signs his yearly Christmas cards as "Frank", but who will really always be Mr. Hoffmeister to me) who headed up the opera theatre, became my mentor. He took me under his wing and was my biggest cheerleader. I worked with him as I accompanied opera theatre rehearsals and productions, and also accompanied several of his vocal students (Frank, himself, had an extraordinary tenor voice!). He was there for me when I became overwhelmed or thought I couldn't do everything I was trying to do. He always told me, "Yes, you can." And somehow, I did.

In my fourth year of college, I gave a senior piano recital, even though I didn't have to as a music minor – this was one of my life-goals! It has – to this day – been one of my biggest achievements. It was an hour long and I played all classical music.

Anyway… this little walk down memory lane was all to tell you how my piano playing has always been a big part of me. However, Greg and I had decided there was no way to take my grand with us as we would not be shipping anything.

With this painful decision made, I focused on the positive. The family who bought it from us was a lovely young couple who had three young daughters – ALL who played piano, and all who played well. Those little girls were so excited about my grand piano; it was really a heart-warming thing to see it go to such a wonderful family. And how thrilling for those girls to grow up learning and practicing on such an amazing instrument! Still, tears were shed when I watched the piano movers pack it up and take it out my front door.

After the piano left the house, our furniture continued to dwindle, little by little, and by the time we moved, we didn't have much left to move to the place we would be renting. We rented a U-Haul and did all the moving ourselves. BIG MISTAKE – both of my thighs displayed a lovely array of black and purple bruises after moving day. Still, I was proud that we were able to move everything without help.

We moved into a tiny rental house a few miles down the street and signed a 6 month lease as we knew we wanted to work through May or June, still stockpiling and saving as much money as we could. Unfortunately, the more Greg worked, the more he just wanted to be done with it already. Greg was thoroughly and completely stressed out, yet needed to keep working for that "little extra bit" of money. This was difficult for me to watch and for us both to get through this time. It seemed like an oxymoron – we were going to be simplifying our lives, but in order for us to do so – we had to break our backs working and stressing out – for just *that little bit more* of money. At least we had an end in sight. It was less than half a year away. Yet knowing this seemed to make it even harder. It was so close, yet seemed so far.

Enter painful decision #2 – Sahara Lucy. What were we going to do with this big girl? Could we bring her to Costa Rica with us? As previously stated – Sahara was not a normal dog – she weighed more than I did! She was a gentle, good, sweet girl, though very confident as well. We couldn't imagine giving her up – especially after we flew to Ohio and rescued her in the first place! However, we had several concerns with taking her to Costa Rica.

We would have to have a customized crate built for her airplane flight (they didn't make them big enough for her 180-pound-size), and we were concerned about the heat and stress of the plane ride in the cargo department (Sahara is a bit skittish). Sahara was also on a raw diet (meaning she ate raw chicken – very healthy for her and her teeth), but the price of chicken in Costa Rica was more expensive than the States.

Also – we found out Costa Rica did not have pet lodges, and we knew we would have to leave the country every 90 days. Who would take care of Sahara when we had to make a border run? We didn't know anyone who we could be assured would watch over her while we were gone.

Sahara also needed to be walked everyday, but I was worried about how we would do this with so many street dogs running around. Sahara was NOT good with other dogs – in fact – she had been kicked out of doggy day care because she could not get along with others well. She was great with humans and kids and babies – but dogs? Nope.

Finally, after we went back and forth for months over this issue, we called the original breeder in Ohio. I was so nervous about this call, but the breeder was down to earth and calm. She listened to us and helped talk us through everything.

Besides the help of the Ohio American Mastiff breeder, we also had help from a new Texas American Mastiff breeder and other American Mastiff owners with whom we had become friends (thanks to an awesome Facebook group!). They ALL helped us tremendously during this painful time. Surprisingly I have remained close with some of these American Mastiff owners to this day, and they have truly become friends.

Once we moved into our temporary rental house, Sahara had a hard time settling in and getting comfortable. I could hardly blame her – our rental place was TINY and NOISY with train tracks right behind our house and lots of dogs in the neighborhood. Sahara did not do well with any of this; she seemed miserable. She was used to peace and quiet and having lots of space in the house to roam around during the day. She was not used to having other dogs bark at her on either side of our back yard, which just had a short chain linked fence, every time she went outside.

After about a year of this guilt, indecisiveness, and constant worrying about Sahara – we finally came to a decision. This could NOT have been done without the help of our extended American Mastiff family.

We decided that it was in Sahara's best interest to try to re-home her in Dallas and not make the move to Costa Rica. Unless, of course, the "right" family could not be found.

I connected more with the Texas American Mastiff breeder who was a tremendous support to me and held my hand during this emotional time. She recommended a family to us who had been looking for an older/adult American Mastiff.

As soon as I contacted this family, it seemed like it was meant to be. They were a couple with a cute little boy, and they all promptly fell in love with Sahara after having her stay with them for a week. They had a spacious home with a huge fenced in backyard and the kicker was – they had an XXL doggie door already built into their laundry room! It didn't take Sahara long to figure this out. They were also game for keeping up her raw food diet, which satisfied us, and Sahara was great with their little boy.

Giving up Sahara was extremely hard on us, but with these people, it was *much less* difficult than it could have been. We knew they loved Sahara, and no matter what, they would take care of her.

They have been awesome to this day. They have kept in touch with me via texts and pictures and, the best part, have given us an open invitation to visit her anytime.

Luckily, those were the only painful decisions for us. I don't think I could have dealt with another one. With both of these resolved, it was time to move forward with wrapping up the rest of our Dallas life.

There was no going back now, and strangely, I was not scared at all.

15. social media, i heart you

Where is Mark Zuckerberg, so I can thank him personally for this fabulous thing he created called Facebook? My hubby found this awesome Facebook group called "Expatriates in Costa Rica." All these expats (whoa – I would be an "expat" soon!) who *lived* in Costa Rica – and there were TONS of them. I thought Greg and I were the only ones! Oddly enough, these people had already DONE what we were going to do. Most of them were even older than us. I seriously respected these people – being of retirement age, and moving from their homeland to a foreign country?? It was hard enough for me at my age; I can't imagine being OLDER and doing it. And here they were, ready and willing, to help us and answer our questions. We had done quite a bit of research already, but we did have some questions about certain things. We were grateful for a few people in particular who reached out to us.

Even though we were pretty sure we wanted to rent a house and to try living without a car, it was good to hear other opinions on these subjects. Here are some examples of other questions we had:

> * To ship or not to ship? (There were several companies who shipped containers, but we needed

to decide if we wanted to ship and pay the costs for the few boxes of stuff we were contemplating shipping.)

* Would we apply for residency right away, or would we leave the country every 3 months for a new "90 day stamp?" (It seemed the responses were about 50/50– those who had applied for residency and those who were making border runs; there were pros and cons to each.)

* If we applied for residency, would we need to use an attorney? (You do not, you can do it on your own, but because neither Greg nor I spoke Spanish, the thought of us doing this on our own was daunting.)

* Did other people have issues with bugs like me, and if so, how did they deal with them? (I didn't find any comfort with this question. Clearly, I would need to deal with this on my own.)

* Could we take any of our framed art with us or would it mold? What about paper books, pictures, sheet music? (We kept hearing paper products did indeed mold after a while, depending on where you lived, so we should bring as little paper as possible. My solution? I turned my favorite pictures into refrigerator magnets!)

One couple from the expat group who had been living in Grecia for the last two years messaged me one day to tell me they were from Dallas, and would be *in* Dallas, visiting, in a few weeks, and did we want to get together for dinner? HECK YES! They were bringing a young tica they had befriended as well. We met at Abuelo's, had a lovely dinner and instantly hit it off with all of them. The tica spoke admirable English, and the expat couple had so many helpful suggestions that I had to start jotting some down in my notebook so I wouldn't forget.

We talked about oodles of things – how Costa Rica was, things they had found different there, certain ways to do things, etc.

For example, they talked about a phone called "Magic Jack," for which you could pay a small fee ($20 or so per year) to make unlimited calls to the U.S. or Canada. It plugs into your computer and works through your Wi-Fi, similar to Skype but without the video.

They also told us about a place in downtown Grecia called Aerocasillas, which is a type of postal facility. You could purchase products online – they would be sent to a place in Florida and then sent to Aerocasillas where you could pick them up (all for a fee, of course).

My eyes lit up at this revelation, as it was a way to receive online packages!

They also told us, "If you see something in the grocery store or department store that you want – buy as many as you can that day! The next day they might be out and you never know when (or if) it will ever be back!"

From our new friends, we heard about a wide diversity of microclimates throughout Costa Rica. Depending on where Costa Ricans live, they experience almost every kind of climate, except for a snowy winter wonderland (which is fine with me). Those who live near the ocean find the temperatures are much hotter and more humid. The central valley with its higher elevations, mountains, volcanoes, hills, ridges, and valleys has cooler temps, yet the climate still varies depending on where you live. For example one mountain ridge could be rainy and cloudy and have severe issues with mold in the rainy season; whereas the next mountain ridge over might not have any issues with mold and might have less rainfall. There are also several areas that are in the rain forest, where it rains almost every day and is much cooler overall. We loved hearing about this great climate diversity in a country that is not much bigger than the state of West Virginia.

At the end of our night, I left thinking, *Man, we have SO much to learn!* But with support from friends like this couple, it would be much easier.

Knowing we had made some good Costa Rican friends through Facebook gave me a warm feeling. I looked forward to meeting more of them in person once we moved there.

Now, you may ask, "Where is *there*?" Where were we going to land and start our new life in Costa Rica?

Actually, I was sold on Grecia the minute I heard that people living there did not have heaters or air conditioning in their homes – you just don't need them! For Greg and me, Grecia had the perfect temperature, year round. Although we are both a little hot natured, we have since met friends who find it "too cold" in Grecia, so it is definitely a personal preference. Also, no heating or air conditioning is easy on the electric bill. Temperatures can drop to the low 60's sometimes at night or in the rainy season, and rarely rise above 80 during the day at the higher elevations. *Grecia Centro* (central downtown) runs about 5 degrees warmer than the surrounding hill areas which tend to be higher in altitude.

After seeing and experiencing Grecia on our trip, we thought it might be a good place for us to start. Grecia has several "ridges" as they call them, which are really mountain ridges that veer out from the city like spokes of a wheel (although not that symmetrical). In between the ridges are valleys which create GORGEOUS views. Each of the ridges are at higher elevations, much higher than *Grecia Centro*, which make for even cooler temperatures. That really appealed to us. Plus, we didn't think we wanted to live downtown anyway – too busy and noisy.

When most people think of Grecia, they think of the large, red church in the center of town, built entirely of prefabricated steel plates, the Iglesia de la Nuestra Señora de las Mercedes, right across from the Central Park. When you ask for directions to any place in Grecia, they all start with, "Well, you know where the church is, right?"

In spite of Grecia's perfect temperatures and its small-town charm, it does *not* attract much tourism. But it had enough of what we needed – several small grocery stores, cafés, banks, even a "mall" which was pretty small but has quite a few clothing shops and a movie theatre. We wanted to live in a "local" place – with not a lot of tourists or tourist shops.

We were not moving to Costa Rica for a vacation – we were going there to *live*. We wanted to try to get to know the ticos and live amongst them as best as we could. Also, Grecia is not too far from one of the international airports, and is also close to the capital city of San José, where we would need to go if we decided to apply for residency.

We figured with the climate, the small-town-ness, the NON-tourism-ness, and the closeness to the airport and San José, Grecia would be the perfect place for us to start our new life.

16. here we go – push me

Before we knew it, when it seemed Greg's job would never end, May 1st was upon us and it was time for us to put in our notices! Greg's boss was downright incredulous, and Greg had to tell him three times before it sank in. My boss was surprised, but then immediately happy for me, wanting to know all the details. Then I told my pal Dave, another manager in my office – he just silently stared at me and let me talk (which was unusual for him). When I finally came to a pause, he said, "So... you're going to go all "granola girl" on us, huh? Go off into the jungle, stop shaving your armpits, make things out of hemp, and grow your hair into dreadlocks?" Well, no, Dave – not quite that dramatic (although I *did* start making homemade granola and bracelets out of hemp...).

Once our notices were given, everything started happening very quickly.

I've told you what a planner/organizer I am, right? So I had planned we would move out of our rental house and stay with Greg's folks for a couple weeks before leaving for Costa Rica. Reasoning? Can you imagine living/eating/showering/sleeping in a house one night, and taking off the next morning with all your belongings to a foreign country?? Way too much stress. Doing it my way would give us time to move out of the rental house and get it cleaned, wrap up our bills, and just give us some time so we could do a "calm transition." I didn't want to be concerned or frazzled with too many last minute things the morning before hopping on a plane to move out of the country!

It worked out great, actually, as we spent two weeks living with Mom and Dad Seymour and had some real quality time with them (unfortunately for Greg, this meant stripping and painting the back deck in 100 degree weather). Also, Greg's sister's family of nine had moved back to Dallas from Hawaii a week before we left, so it was really great to hang with them. Yes, we were ALL in the same little house together for a while... not sure how we all fit, but we made it work.

The day before we left was spent fine tuning our packing and weighing each of the *nine* pieces of luggage on a scale; each piece could not be over 50 pounds. Greg did much reorganizing of items to redistribute the weight, all with a smile on his face. We had found out it would have been much more cost efficient to purchase business class airline tickets, which would have given us three free checked pieces of luggage each at a 70 pound weight limit, instead of the one suitcase each with a limit of 50 pounds that we were allowed with the coach fare. We were on the waiting list to be upgraded for business class, but this never became available for us. We ended up with two carry-ons and seven pieces of checked luggage, which cost us a total of $530.00 in extra baggage fees. This was ALL we were taking with us, as we were not shipping anything separately.

Just imagine, our whole life and 18 years of marriage... packed into nine pieces of luggage! Surreal. Very surreal.

Before we knew it, it was June 17th and we were standing on the Seymours' driveway with our horde of luggage, ready to make our way to the airport!

YIKES! It was hard to believe that we were REALLY doing this!! But this was happening, whether I believed it or not.

Costa Rica – ready or not, here we come!

PART IV – LIVING THE DREAM

17. the bird has landed

How many times, back in the States, had someone asked me nonchalantly, "Hey Jen-Jen, what ya been up to lately?" and I would answer "Oh, you know, just living the dream." Said sarcastically, of course.

What was so positively coined as the "American Dream" in the 1950's and 60's had somehow, now-a-days, come to mean: working a crazy-busy job, having an oversized house, multiple cars and expensive toys, spending lots of money and having lots of debt. I was giving up *all* of those things – and it felt great.

And now – here we were! Really and truly on our way to "living the dream." Funny how the more positive notion of "living the dream" for me, now, was going to be in Costa Rica – CENTRAL America, not North America. I could barely wrap my head around the concept.

Greg and I were both excited and anxious. I don't mean anxious in a bad way, as I knew what we were getting into. I truly felt prepared and confident that we were fully equipped with the knowledge to get us past the "hard times" that for sure would come up, enough so that we could enjoy all the good things Costa Rica would have to offer.

We had found a place up in the foothills above Grecia, where we would be staying for the first 3 months. It was a large house, split up into 5 separate apartments. Small pool. Gorgeous views of the central valley. Lots of fruit trees and flowers. We were to occupy a small one-bedroom, which was fully furnished, including all utilities (electric, water, cable and Wi-Fi). We knew it would be the perfect landing spot for us while we took our time to find a bigger, more private place to live. In my super-organized state before we arrived, I emailed quite a bit with the landlord, as he would be picking us up from the airport.

In my final emails, days before our arrival, I asked him if he wanted a picture of us.

"No" (he was not a man of many words).

I replied, concerned, "But, how will you know who we are?"

"Jen, who else will be arriving with 9 pieces of luggage?" Ah, good point.

At DFW airport, we were able to check in all of our bags curbside, which was a huge relief to us! DFW had just recently started allowing curbside check-ins for international flights and we were happy to take advantage of this. Our load was lightened almost immediately. We checked in seven bags and were left with two small ones to carry on, along with two personal items, which were our backpacks.

Sitting at our gate, having gotten our boarding passes and gone through security, texts with family done, Facebook updated… we had nothing left to do but anxiously await the call to board.

And then – we were notified that our flight was delayed… .

Seriously? The "rest of our life" was suddenly delayed? This was kind of excruciating… after having waited SO long for this moment. A year and a half of decisions and planning and organizing and selling and keeping secrets – just to wait a bit longer.

Ah well, we figured it was meant to be. On the bright side, we got to practice tico time a bit. We settled in, relaxed, and read our books.

Then – *another* flight delay – #2.

This time, off we went to an Irish Restaurant located in our terminal and had a glass of wine and something to eat (the food compliments of American Airlines, as they pass out dining vouchers after the second delay), and tried to relax and be patient. We were excited to get on with our life, but nervous about getting through customs, and to be honest – just being able to *carry* everything. Nine pieces of luggage is a lot, and we didn't know if they even had luggage carriers in Costa Rica, let alone if you had to pay for them in the local currency of colones (which we did not have yet). Yep, I worry a lot… .

Then – *another* flight delay – #3.

Well, what could we do? Nothing but wait.

Another glass of wine and several hours later – we finally got called to board our flight. Once we finally took off from DFW, everything with the flight went splendidly. We arrived in Costa Rica a bit later than planned (instead of 9 pm that night, it was 1:30 the next morning), but customs was a breeze, they DID have luggage carriers, and they were FREE!

Our new landlord picked us up at the airport exit, loaded us into a van and drove the 45-minute trip to our new, albeit temporary, "home." During the trip, we saw lightening storms in the distance, even though it was not raining where we were. Welcome to Costa Rica and – the rainy season!

There were a few surprises… like turning down the gravel, heavily pot-holed road that led to the place we would be staying. It was NOT a smooth road. Once we got there, we found that "our place" wasn't quite ready yet. The couple staying in it, who should have left that morning, would not be leaving until early the next morning. We were put in a small guest room with a private bath, which was fine, actually – we were so tired we were asleep in no time. Pura vida!

The next morning our landlord made us some delicious coffee, and we sat outside by the pool that overlooked the central valley.

It was gorgeous! We really *were* in paradise!

The view from the pool, looking out over a huge valley, was breathtaking. Surrounding the pool were tall fruit trees, flowers and tropical bushes. There were hummingbirds everywhere. The sun was rising, but it was cool with a comfortable breeze. We met two other couples sitting there having coffee; one from Texas, y'all, one from Minnesota, ya know, and Greg and I felt at home right away.

Our landlord took us into town later that morning to a grocery store, while our place was cleaned and readied for our return. We then moved into our new "home".

We had arrived!

18. trouble in paradise

The first couple of days, we settled into our apartment, unpacked a bit, stocked up on groceries, met our neighbors, and spent a sufficient amount of time sipping coffee down by the pool overlooking the valley.

Our third morning in Costa Rica, I was in the kitchen pouring myself a cup of coffee when Greg walked in from the bedroom.

"Um, Jen… I don't want you to be alarmed or anything… ."

Me, pouring coffee into my cup: "OK… what??"

"I think I just got stung by a scorpion."

"WHAT?????" I screamed, "Where is he??"

Turned out the scorpion was STILL in the bedroom and was ALIVE and KICKING! I instantly ran to get the duct tape (note – not much regard for my hubby who had just been stung, I was all about catching and killing that scorpion *first*).

Our friend Rachelle had taught me this duct tape trick to catch and kill a scorpion – which of course, I had previously shown to Greg and had him review and memorize each step before we left the States – all in preparation of coming into contact with our first scorpion. This scorpion turned out to be a dark colored "little guy" by scorpion standards, about 1.5 – 2" long. Greg followed the instructions he had memorized and promptly stuck him with the tape, folded the tape on top of him, and wacked him with a shoe. End of story!

During all this chaos there was a knock at the door, and I opened it to find a man standing there with a three-foot-long machete: "Did someone scream??"

It turned out to be our marine-corps-neighbor, Joe, standing there, ready to help. Thanks, Joe.

The scorpion sting turned out to be not too bad – Greg said a bee sting hurt worse. He had already done research and found that there are no poisonous scorpions in Costa Rica, and after about an hour he couldn't even see or feel the sting.

That was our first scorpion experience. The scorpion had been in some shorts Greg had tossed on the floor a day earlier. So now, we're very careful and don't leave anything on the floor, and we always check all of our clothes and shoes, regardless of where they are before putting them on.

After we calmed down, we refreshed our coffee mugs and went outside by the pool to sip coffee with our neighbors, and talk about our first scorpion experience. Pura vida!

19. more trouble in paradise

After shooting the breeze with our neighbors about the scorpion, we came back inside for more coffee. We noticed Greg's sister Misty had tried to call us, and had left an urgent sounding message to call her ASAP. Greg instantly had a bad feeling.

Our phone that we had set up with Magic Jack was not working perfectly yet, so it took us a while, but finally we connected with Misty.

Greg's dad had just passed away.

He either had a heart attack or a stroke, and the ambulance had just left with him. The paramedics had tried to revive him for a long time, and before that Brady, Misty's husband, had performed CPR; but it was all to no avail. Richard was now gone. We were all in shock.

Our world shifted. We *knew* Richard was in bad health, and this could happen at any moment, but he'd been home from his long hospital stay (heart attack, diabetes, kidney failure) for three months now, and was seemingly "back in the flow of things". Although, when we really thought about it, he did NOT have his strength back. In fact, he was worn out by very small things – both emotionally and physically. And the 4-

times-a-week trips to dialysis were really taking their toll on him. He was just so exhausted, seemingly, with just *living* day to day.

In hindsight, I truly believe he felt *good* about his family and the life he had lived, and he was "okay to go." The weekend before he passed, he had an amazing Father's Day, where his *whole* family had been with him. Greg and I were already living there. His daughter Misty and her family had just returned from a 6-month mission trip in Hawaii. His son Michael, Jenni and family, and son Marty, Kim and family were there with all of us for Father's Day. So, all in all, he had just seen all of his normally scattered family, and was feeling satisfied with everyone. He was just too weak, heart-wise and physically, to continue any longer.

I had an extremely good relationship with him, which I feel I need to point out, because after all I am his *daughter-in-law*. You never really hear about people honestly *loving* their in-laws. Well, I do – both Richard and Shirley! When my girlfriends would complain about their husbands' families, as they often would, I would just sit there and listen… and listen. And then finally would tell them about how great I have it, and they would stare at me in open-eyed-disbelief. No one would ever believe me when I said that honestly, I had no problems with my in-laws.

Richard was truly an awesome man. And he wasn't just "nice" to me – he truly loved me for who I was, and also loved talking to me and emailing with me. He was incredibly sweet to me always. He loved that his son married me, and how great of a compliment is that?

I had sent him a long email the day before he died, as I knew he loved getting emails from me. He had responded to me just an *hour*(!) before he passed away that morning and told me he loved hearing my stories and all about our day in Costa Rica. What an awesome parting gift to me.

Greg and I had also Face-Timed with him just two days before, so I felt this was really good for Greg… to have talked with Dad, let him know we were doing well in Costa Rica and were settled and happy.

So – after one week of living in Costa Rica – we flew back to Dallas and spent two weeks with Greg's mom and his sister's family, helping where we could. It was good to be living with my seven nieces and nephews; they gave us comic relief when we needed it most. I'll never forget one morning how 6-year-old Edie, when asked by her mom to pick up the room, put her hand on her hip and stated most emphatically, "Why am *I* the only one who *ever* does any work around here?" Oh, Edie… you make my heart smile.

We planned and attended Richard's memorial service, which was the BEST service I'd ever been to. So upbeat, with good stories and funny memories spoken of him by many people. It was amazing. To laugh more than you cry at a funeral, that is truly a sign of a good service. It was such an awesome and deserving tribute to my Dad #2.

"Dad #2" is the name Richard gave himself after my dad died, as he knew he couldn't replace my dad, but wanted to be a "Second Dad" to me. See what I mean? He was so incredibly sweet.

Rest in peace now, Dad #2. No more exhaustion or suffering for you.

20. costa rica – take two

We returned to Costa Rica after two weeks in Dallas. It was good to be back to our new home.

We were still at our temporary place, which was a tiny, 450 square-foot, one-bedroom apartment with a mini-kitchenette. Think half-everything: half size refrigerator, half size stove/oven. We felt on top of each other all the time (even when we weren't in the bedroom). We had nowhere to store our 9 suitcases, so they were standing along a wall, which lead to endless tripping and toe-stubbing. At least on my part, I'm pretty klutzy.

But, all smallness aside, we couldn't have asked for a better starting place – the scenery, nature, views, and fruit trees – all of it was ideal. We planned to keep our eyes and ears open for a more permanent place to live.

It was good to settle into a "routine" – if you could call it that. We always woke up early with the sun (5:30 ish), and then drank massive quantities of coffee by the pool while enjoying the view and chatting with our fellow neighbors. As our three-month period continued, our neighbors changed and we met new people.

Later in the morning, we would usually go for a long hike. The rest of the day we played by ear. Sometimes we went into town for groceries or errands, which usually took up most of the afternoon with the bus ride in and back. We also spent time writing for our blogs, which were now both up and running. Sometimes we would get together with our neighbors and have dinner or drinks, or go into town. Each day was fun and different and held endless possibilities. I loved having a "blank" calendar for once in my life.

Some of the people we had met on the Facebook Expat Group happened to live in Grecia. They started contacting us, wanting to meet in town for lunch or dinner to welcome us to town and show us around, and we soon found ourselves… well, almost busy! Upon our return from Dallas, during our first two weeks back, we were meeting someone for lunch almost every other day. We were welcomed by these new friends, and they helped us tremendously in our first few weeks here. They answered our questions, showed us around, and told us about the ins and outs of things. For example: how to ride the bus, where to find a dentist or doctor, and where to eat good typical Costa Rican food. Many of these initial "Facebook acquaintances" have become truly good real-life friends.

One such couple took us to a fabulous little cozy restaurant up one of the other ridges, called Isabel's. It's actually called Ezzpresso de la Casa, but everyone just calls it Isabel's. Isabel is the chef and owner, and she is as sweet as her food is delicious. She is originally from Mexico, and serves her food with a definite Mexican flair. Greg, of course, was in heaven from the first bite (if he could, he would eat Mexican food every day of his life). A lot of people seem to think Costa Rica is flush with Mexican food, but this is not the case because this is Costa Rica, not Mexico. Costa Rican food is very different from Mexican food – it is typically fairly bland, and is usually served with a lot of rice, beans, plantain, avocado and fruit. There is virtually no Mexican food to be found in Grecia except at Isabel's. Isabel even had a special hot sauce suitable for Greg's hunkering for heat. She also makes amazing coffee, lattes and hot chocolate, hence the name of her restaurant. Her prices are reasonable, and it's BYOB (which could stand for "bring your own box" – more on that later). It was such a fun overall experience going to her place. In the coming days and months, we ventured to her place several times, with different people, and once even by ourselves for a special date!

We also discovered, from one friend or another, different small cafés (called *sodas*) in town. Every soda we have tried has had good typical Costa Rican food. There is also a small mall here, which, get this – has a food court just like the USA(!): KFC, McDonald's, Pizza Hut, Taco Bell. Ugh, I was so dismayed to see this! We try to stay away from the fast food as much as possible, plus it is very expensive. You can get so much more for your money at a soda, and even *more* for your money at the local farmer's market.

Here are some examples of what you can get for **$7.00 (or 3,500 colones)** at various eateries:

KFC: A combo meal of chicken fingers, fries & a soft drink

A typical café (soda): A "casado" AND an bottle of Imperial – which is the national beer of Costa Rica.

At the local farmer's market (feria):

2 heads of organic lettuce

2 mangoes

1 bag of mora berries (sort of like a tart blackberry)

2 medium pineapples

5 avocados

1 large bag of tiny potatoes

1 loaf of French bread

The feria is obviously your best bet for the money. It is the local weekend farmer's market and is open on Friday afternoon/evening and Saturday morning. IT IS FABULOUS. They have rows and rows of fresh fruits, vegetables, meat, organic coffee, bakery items, clothes, shoes, flowers – almost anything you want! Plus a couple of places to eat a quick lunch or have an awesome fresh fruit drink. YUM. Of course, there are little fruit/veggie stands everywhere around Grecia, but this is the "king of all farmers' markets" on the weekend, which everyone waits for.

There is one stand at the feria that has really good fresh baked bread, and the owner happens to be a gringo. One thing I need to mention here is that the Costa Rican breads and pastries are dissimilar from that which we eat in the States. They seem to be dry and lacking in flavor and consistency – they taste more like plain, simple, well… cardboard, actually. Just kind of – blah. The smell of the *Panadería* (bakery) and the look of the breads and pastries gives false hope for the bread and pastry connoisseur.

This started me thinking about making my own bread. I mean – why not? You could get flour and yeast at the grocery store, right? Why not give it a try? My wheels began spinning… .

21. éclairs

Speaking of bread and pastries… my éclairs were something that I had wanted to try, ever since we had returned to Costa Rica from our emergency trip to Dallas. I was both excited *and* nervous about trying them. Nervous because I wasn't sure I could obtain all the ingredients I was used to using. Also the oven we had in our teeny-tiny temporary place had a dial that, instead of numbered temperature settings, had only "warm, grill, high-bake, or low-bake." This could be a recipe for disaster!

Back in the States, I loved to bake and always made a dessert whenever I needed to bring something for a dinner or party. I don't know why or how or when this came about. I remember growing up and *never* wanting to help my mom in the kitchen (sorry, Mom, you had one daughter and she never wanted to bake or cook growing up when I'm sure you could have used the help!). I must have started to like baking after I got married – as Greg does not remember being wooed by my sweets.

My éclairs, back in my early-married days, were my "go-to" recipe, if I ever needed to make a dessert. It was a recipe handed down from my Aunt Barb to my mom and then to me. It was a recipe I actually *enjoyed* making and even better than that, was having people sincerely love them!

As I gained confidence, I tried different desserts and found people always enjoyed them. Before I knew it, I was looking forward to events so that I could try something new. I think the most amazing thing to me was that I used to view baked goods as something someone else did, not me. I couldn't even envision myself making them. But then I started to experiment and realized I was actually good at baking – and I enjoyed it too!

In Costa Rica, some of the ingredients were slightly different, and other ingredients you just couldn't get here, at least not in our small town of Grecia – things like Cool Whip and Jell-O Instant Pudding, both of which I needed for my simple éclair recipe.

Although I had brought a box of Jell-O Instant Pudding with me from the States, I soon found that there is *no* Cool Whip here. Real cream (heavy or half-and-half, like we are used to in the States) is hard to find here; the only place to buy it is from actual dairy farmers. But Costa Rica has something here called *Crema Dulce* that you can whip into whipped cream – but I'm not really sure what it IS exactly. It is sold in the grocery stores on the shelf in a small box, NOT refrigerated, and has a *very* long shelf life. Another thing was that the butter seemed different here; it was very yellow in color, more like margarine, although it was labeled as "real butter." It would have to suffice, as butter is a necessary ingredient for my choux pastries (the pastry part of an éclair). I was looking forward to trying my éclairs, but was nervous about how they would turn out with these different ingredients and the non-degreed oven.

Yea! They turned out great! Our friends and neighbors all loved them. I was a happy camper.

After that initial success, I focused on making the custard completely from scratch, using only those ingredients that I could find in my small town. After spending time on some different methods and recipes for homemade custard, I finally put together one that my friends and I simply love (see bonus chapter at the end for my éclair recipe!).

I had feared moving to Costa Rica would mean catastrophe for my favorite recipes. Instead, it was the best thing that could have happened! Now, I use more authentic, more healthy ingredients.

I had so much fun experimenting with my éclairs, and making the recipe truly my own. I couldn't wait to try another recipe!

22. getting comfortable with uncomfortable firsts

Living in a new country meant that we experienced many new uncomfortable "firsts." Just as I did when I baked my first éclairs in Costa Rica, I kept reminding myself that these uncomfortable firsts were also brave new adventures!

Shortly after we returned from Dallas, we had one of these "firsts:" our first bus ride!

Our initial bus ride was with our new neighbors because without them as our guide, we would have been even more apprehensive about the whole process: how do we pay, when do we pull the cord, where is the cord, when does the bus come, where do we stand, etc. It doesn't sound that difficult, right? Being in a foreign country puts an extra layer of fear on things, at least for me. Not only do we not speak the language, but sadly, public transportation had never been a part of our lives – I would have felt apprehensive catching the bus in Dallas.

The short trip into town, which was nine miles long and took 35 minutes, cost only 420 colones per person (about $0.85). The bus trip ended in *Grecia Centro* at the bus station that serves all of Grecia and several other towns. We found out that there are yellow strips, painted on the road about every 50 meters, and that is where you can stand and wait for the bus. When you get on the bus, you pay with colones to the driver – he has a change box with him and will give you change if needed. The cord is located on each side of the bus near the roof above the windows. When you pull the cord, a sound is made, and the driver is notified by a light on his dashboard. No credit cards or advance tickets. If you are a senior (age 65 and over with Costa Rican residency) or a child (three years and under) – you ride free.

After we arrived in town, we walked around the park for a bit, went to the grocery store, and then visited the central market (*centro mercado*). The *centro mercado* is downtown next to the bus station, all covered, but with individual stands. Sometimes it smells like garbage, but other times it smells fresh and wonderful. Here you can find most anything you'd want – fruits, veggies, meat, baking supplies, macrobiotic stores, and also little *sodas* – with stools to sit on at a small bar and eat. There are several stalls selling fresh meat and cheese. I watched in fascination as a man climbed into the back of a refrigerated truck parked just outside, threw an entire pig carcass over his shoulder, and delivered it to one of the butchers!

After we explored for a bit, we met up with our neighbors, and had lunch at a restaurant a couple of blocks from the *centro mercado*. We both had a *casado* and mine was VERY good and filling; I couldn't eat half of it! Cost: about $5 each.

A few days later, Greg and I took the bus by ourselves. We were fine going into town, but as we were coming home it started to rain. Shortly after the rain began, I looked out the window but couldn't see anything – the cloud forest was upon us! It WAS the rainy season (May – November) and we had heard about the ominous "cloud forest." The cloud forest happens in parts of the central valley when it rains or before it rains. It is a thick, dense fog that moves in quickly so that you cannot see anything. We weren't able to see any landmarks and I wasn't even sure how the bus driver could be driving through this cloud forest!

Our nervousness must have been apparent, as all of a sudden, someone tugged my sleeve. I turned around and found this cute, petite tica who was sitting behind me, already starting to talk to me. She used a combination of Spanish and English – and she was so sweet. She was asking me where we lived so she could help us know when to pull the cord. She kept talking to me, and even though she was trying to reassure us, I couldn't help but become more and more nervous. When someone is talking to me, I have to give that person eye contact. It's just what I do. So of course, I couldn't look out the window AND look her in the eye while she was talking. Greg was glancing out the window from time to time, but I couldn't totally rely on him.

This was our first dose of the Costa Rican kindness… something we would come to find everywhere here. She ended up getting off before us after showering us with many smiles and goodbyes and good lucks and don't worries.

Amazingly enough, the fog seemed to clear a bit and a familiar landmark appeared before us. We were able to pull the cord and get off right at our heavily-pot-holed-dirt-road! I was so relieved! We then walked down the road for a half mile in the pouring rain with our reusable grocery bags before arriving home... wet and thoroughly exhausted. But do you think I cared? It *was* the rainy season, and I was just happy we had made it off the bus at the right stop! Pura vida.

The bus wasn't the only thing we were uncomfortable with at first. We were very nervous about going to the grocery store for the first time by ourselves.

Almost all stores here in Costa Rica seem to have lockers or cubbyholes with a person watching your goods. They are in the front of each store and offer two purposes: it lightens your load while shopping, and also helps prevent stealing (the latter being the main purpose, I'm sure). But what if there were no lockers left? And if we tried to carry our bags into the store with us, would we be reprimanded (in Spanish!)? What about remembering the conversion for colones to dollars? What about checking out at the register? What if they speak Spanish to us while checking out? What will we say? How will we respond?

As it happened, on our first trip to the grocery store, we had no problems. We found a locker and easily figured it out (close door, turn to lock and take key!). Thanks to Greg, I always had a walking money-conversion-calculator with me (and also someone to remind me if something was too expensive to buy). The cashier was friendly and helpful, *and* happened to speak a bit of English!

See, everything worked out just fine... we just had to get through that "first uncomfortable-ness." The next time at the store, we felt even more confident, especially after learning some more Spanish phrases. And now it's absolutely no big deal at all. Pura vida!

Another uncomfortable first... going into a Bank! Banks here are... well, just a bit different than in the States.

Upon going in the front door, you first have to wait in front of an "isolation booth" until the light turns green.

At that point, a glass door slides open, you enter one person at a time and stand very still (just like at the airport). The door closes behind you while the glass door in front remains closed. You hold open any bags you have, and a guard with a gun looks inside them. They then "approve" you (hopefully) and the last glass door slides open, allowing you entrance into the bank. Furthermore, you cannot wear hats or sunglasses and must not use your cell phone unless you want to have your wrist slapped.

Once you are inside (and this can take a while), you then have to pull a number, just like at a meat counter, then take a seat and wait for your number to be called. This is all just to see a teller. There is quite a bit of business that still takes place at banks in Costa Rica and it is not uncommon to have 20 or 30 people ahead of you in line. Unlike my bank in Dallas that usually has one teller available, here there will be five or six tellers taking care of the patrons.

The first time we did all this, let me tell you, it was scary and more than just uncomfortable (and we probably looked guilty as heck). Luckily, we knew what to expect, as we had a couple of friends forewarn us, but still – to see a place flanked with guards and their heavy-looking machine guns (well, they *look* like machine guns) watching your every move… it is unnerving.

However, it made a lot sense to me after I thought about it. Banks SHOULD be overly protective of who they allow inside! Definitely these isolation booths would weed out anyone with guns or explosives… just a thought.

23. getting into a routine

The more "uncomfortable firsts" we got out of the way, the more relaxed we became and settled into a routine with our new life.

One activity that quickly became a part of our new life was hiking. We soon developed a habit of hiking every morning. We would always get up early, around 5:30 or so, as the sun would have already risen at that time and the birds would be chirping. We would have our coffee by the pool, visit with our neighbors, and enjoy the view and nature. Then, a bit later, we would head out for our hike.

One of our favorite hikes was to continue on the road that our apartment was on to where most people think it dead-ends; it really just turns from a road into a dirt trail. It can be pretty muddy and slippery in places, if it rained the day before, and the road has lots of rocks and roots to trip on. Surprisingly, I haven't tripped or fallen yet. The route goes through a coffee farm (*finca*) – up, up, up (*arriba, arriba, arriba*) providing us with gorgeous, breathtaking views that beg to be stopped and looked at. That works out perfectly for me when I'm trying to actually catch my breath.

There are leaf cutter ants everywhere! We are always careful to watch for them and not get in their way. They are easy to pick out because they are always carrying bright green pieces of leaves. They are hard-working and march in single file. It's odd how we can watch them for a long time without getting bored. I often worry about what happens to them on these trails when it rains – the rain must wash them and all their hard work down the mountain. How frustrating!

In addition to ants, we have seen numerous fruit trees on this hike: banana, orange, avocado and *limón*. Most lemons, called *limones* here, are green on the outside and orange on the inside. They taste more like a lime than a lemon, but not quite as sour. You can grow yellow lemons here, but they are rarely seen, and the ticos prefer the limons. I never tire of seeing all these fruits growing naturally here!

The trail from the coffee finca comes out higher up on "the Main Cajón road" – which is the only name I've heard our main road called. There are no street signs anywhere. The hike leads back down this road until we return to the road our apartment is on. The whole hike is about 1.5 miles. Our neighbor Joe showed this route to Greg – and the first time Greg did it, it took him over an hour. He was not in good shape, he had a cold at the time, and he had also just heard about his dad's death – he struggled to complete it. However, by the end of our three-month stay, Greg was doing this hike in less than 30 minutes and had lost 30 pounds!

After his dad passed away, Greg started taking some longer hikes by himself, venturing onto different roads and finding different paths. This was good quiet time for him and he was hiking more miles in shorter time frames every day. Just a note: there are NO flat areas here in Grecia – especially up on the El Cajón ridge where we live. So in addition to having a good mileage hike, we also work different muscles all the time either going up or down very steep hills.

What's the very best part of taking a long hard hike and getting hot? Cooling off in the pool afterwards! The place we were staying had a small rectangular pool (I especially liked the smallness of the pool – I could say I swam "50 laps" and people would be super impressed). After one such hike, Greg and I were swimming (okay, floating) in the pool, and our neighbor Joe and his son came out and chatted with us. We soon started talking about fruit, since the pool area was surrounded with rich fruit trees, and his son started picking fruit for us to try. He brought back a small mandarin-looking orange. And I replied, "Thanks, I'll try it later."

Marine-corps-Joe whipped out his pocket knife and said, "What do you mean later? Let's peel this baby up right now!"

He then (quite expertly I might add) peeled an orange and handed it to me. Yuuuuuum – delicious!!

His son was in full swing now, picking every kind of fruit he could find for us. He handed a mango to his dad, and Joe promptly and efficiently (what exactly did he DO in the Marines?) peeled the mango and sliced off a huge chunk and handed it to me.

OMG – this mango was delicious! It was soft, juicy, a little tart, and bursting with flavor. I thought maybe I could live on a diet of fruit alone (well, plus coffee). Also, what's better than hanging out in a pool and having people pick fruit and peel it for you?

Another part of my routine soon became going to yoga. I had always wanted to try yoga. Of course, back in the States, I'd never had any time for this. In anticipation of having more time, I had even made room for two yoga mats in the nine suitcases we brought. I had great hopes for Greg and myself.

I had seen signs for "yoga" on our road, but still wasn't sure where or when these classes actually were. Then one of my newfound friends emailed me that she knew of someone who went to yoga somewhere near where I lived. I emailed this person, and she told me the class time and days. It turns out, the yoga class was held just up a steep driveway across the road from where we were staying.

Greg preferred to stay home with his yoga mat (he was not being very flexible!), so I found myself nervously going alone to the class. I have been known to be anxious in new situations, which was actually sort of funny... I mean, how did someone like me end up moving from the USA to Costa Rica? Chuckling about that actually helped me calm my nerves.

I walked up the steep hill to the house where the yoga signs pointed. The driveway led to a door, which I promptly knocked on, panting and out of breath from my mountain climb. A beautiful, kind-looking young tica opened the door and told me I had come to the *back* door. (SIGH). But no worries, come in, come in... .

It turned out I was the ONLY person at yoga class that day, which actually worked in my favor. I spent some time in the kitchen, talking to the yoga instructor, and we got to know each other a little bit.

We then went out on her front porch to go over some yoga moves, and WOW. Her porch was large enough to hold a class of 20 people. The beautiful, panoramic view of the Central Valley took my breath away. It was quiet except for the breeze and a flock of parrots occasionally flying by. This was the PERFECT place to do yoga!

After an hour of going over her typical yoga moves and relaxation techniques, I knew I would like this class. I already liked the instructor. What a great experience.

Oh – was I actually nervous before, when I was walking up to class? So silly.

I loved yoga, and it soon became part of my weekly routine.

24. budgeting

Another part of our routine was getting to know our monthly budget. One of the reasons we moved to Costa Rica was to live smaller and more simply. We wanted to get out of the "more more more" mentality (more money, more stuff, etc.), and concentrate on the important things. Of course, quitting our jobs also meant we must learn to live on less money.

After being here for a couple of months, I was ready to try a budget for a whole month to see how little we could get by on. Luckily for me, Greg is ALL about saving money (well, as long as it doesn't cut into his being able to go out for lunch and have a beer once in a while). So, I created a budget, which included some extra money for a few lunches out, since we didn't want to totally deny ourselves something if the opportunity arose.

So – here you have it. We budgeted $1,200.00 for one month, and this is what we itemized it on:

$550.00 – Rent (including water, electricity, cable, Wi-Fi)

$320.00 – Groceries/Farmer's Market

$40.00 – Bus

$40.00 – Yoga

$40.00 – House cleaner once a week (including 2 loads of laundry)

$20.00 – Cell phone minutes for both of us *

$190.00 – Extra (lunches out, etc.)

TOTAL: $1,200.00

At the end of the month, what we *actually* spent was just a little bit under the $1,200.00, and we moved a few dollars around from one category to another. For instance, we only used $4.00 of the $20.00 we had set aside for our cell phones.

A quick note about our cell phones – Greg and I had both kept our iPhone 4S's, which we had unlocked before leaving the States, and then purchased local phone numbers here that came with minutes and a SIM card (at a whopping $2.00 each). Now, we just refill our pay-as-you-go minutes about once a month at $2.00 each, and the minutes last us about a month. When our minutes get low, we just add additional minutes, which you can do most anywhere in town: the grocery store, bus stop, or at a convenience store. Our phones also work for the Internet, even when we are away from a Wi-Fi area, and it doesn't seem to take from our minutes. $2 a month cell phone bill in

Costa Rica, compared to $100 in the States? I'll take it, thank you very much!

Even with this much smaller budget, we didn't feel like we were denying ourselves too much; but at the same time, we were trying to live frugally. One way we saved money on groceries was to buy mainly fresh foods and to eat at home on most days.

I also started cooking and baking more than ever before, which saved us money as well. While chatting with my friend Emma on the bus one day, I became more and more intrigued about the idea of making things from scratch.

Emma is a cool, young, hip mom of two who was living here with her husband and within walking distance down the road from me. She had been telling me about this pizza place she had tried in town and ended by saying, "But actually I like my pizza even better."

"What do you mean, *your* pizza?"

"Oh, well, I make my own."

"You do?? Details, please!"

Upon further discussion, I came to find out she made several other items from scratch besides her pizza:

tomato sauce, bread, cinnamon rolls and yogurt, to name a few! I was amazed.

And the best part? She kept telling me that I could do it too, which I didn't believe at first, but the more I thought about it.... Well, why not try?

She sent me a few recipes that she liked, and voila! I tried them, and I *could* do it too! Greg's dinners suddenly started looking up. I began my "homemade" kick in earnest, studying recipes on the Internet and YouTube and mixing and matching different recipes.

Before I knew it, I had tried pizza dough, tomato sauce, and bread. The bread – ohmygod – was so good, the first loaf I made was actually devoured within minutes. I told you how bland the bread is in Costa Rica, so my new cooking-from-scratch cured this problem. Instead of buying something that doesn't even taste that good, I'll just bake my own. It's fun, I have the time, it saves money, it tastes fresh, it's a great sense of accomplishment, and my hubby loves it! Win – win – win – win!

My hyperactive mind was already envisioning the *"Costa Rica Chica Cookbook."* Sometimes I can be as big a dreamer as my husband....

25. grocery stores

Grecia has several small grocery stores but not a huge selection of things at any one place. The exception to that being TANG. There is quite literally an entire aisle dedicated to Tang powder packets, in every flavor imaginable and in any given grocery store. It's kind of like the Kool-Aid or McCormick seasoning aisles in the States – but supersized.

There are some larger grocery stores farther away from Grecia that have a more North American flair. Automercado, for example, is owned by a gringo and is a famous chain here, where gringos can get their fix of home – although nostalgia is expensive. You can get a lot of things there that we are used to in the States, like Dr. Pepper, imported beers, Ivory Dish Soap, gourmet cheeses, canned pumpkin, even Johnsonville Brats and Feta Cheese from Wisconsin! All for a price, of course. But, Automercado is not in Grecia; it is about a half hour drive to the closest one.

The only way to get heavy cream, like we are used to in the States, is either from a dairy farm or *el hombre de la leche* (the milk man). The milkman drives up and down the roads, delivering fresh milk. In the beginning I wasn't sure how to become a patron of his service; however; just the other day, he stopped by my neighbor's house! I jumped up – got some cash and a pitcher – and ran down to buy some milk. He looked happy to see me, went to the back of his truck, and with a big ladle, scooped out fresh milk from one of his vats (surrounded by ice) into my pitcher. The cost was $1.20 for a liter. It is straight from the cow, none of the homogenized or pasteurized stuff. I promptly poured myself a glass, and it did not disappoint – cold and creamy. I don't think I'll ever have skim milk again in my life if I can help it. I mean, why? The next morning I scraped off some cream that had risen to the top and had some in my coffee – pure deliciousness!

I just recently learned from a friend – who just happens to be a chef-extraordinaire and former restaurant/vineyard owner – of a heavier/thicker cream you *can* find here, called *natilla*! Most people think natilla is Costa Rica's version of sour cream, but really it is a lightly soured heavy cultured cream, similar to crème fraîche. Natilla has a much lower fat content than sour cream (about 12%) and is more creamy and not quite as solid as the sour cream found in the States.

The stores may not have cream like we are used to, but they *all* have a junk food aisle. Grocery stores have a good bit of "American junk food", but most of it is imported (from North America, of course!), and as a result is much more expensive. We try to stay away from the soda and chips aisle in the stores as much as possible. The yogurt is good (although I'm thinking about making my own!). Eggs are sold at room temperature and do not need to be refrigerated. Sometimes people also leave milk out, but I put it in the fridge along with the eggs – I'm a creature of habit.

Greg is used to spicy food, but the typical Costa Rican foods are bland. Greg has found a hot sauce here that he likes to spice up his food. Oddly enough it is called "Tabasco" – but it is *not* your typical Tabasco from Louisiana that is sold in the States. The brand is Lizano, and the name of the sauce is "Tabasco." It is thicker, and spicier. He puts it on everything.

There is cheese in the grocery store, but not a lot of variety like I'm used to, and it is expensive. We try to lay low on the cheese because it costs about two times as much as in the States. We have tried some of the local cheeses but they are very bland. You *can* get cheddar cheese in the store, but a decent size block (size of my hand) is almost $12! I am a Wisconsin-Cheesehead-Girl at heart, so sometimes I have to break my own rule and just buy some good cheese.

A funny thing in the grocery stores here is the bonus deals they have. In the States, you know how stores sometimes have "special bonus" deals with certain products? Like:

– Buy a bottle of Shampoo and get a bottle of Conditioner for FREE (savings of $6!!)!

– Buy bottle of Sunscreen and get a FREE lipgloss tube with SPF 15!

They are usually always pre-packaged by the manufacturer, and of course there's a sign on the packaging that tells you all about the GREAT DEAL you are getting. Actually, it's a great marketing tool and the "bonus deal" you get always compliments the product they are trying to sell.

Here in Costa Rica, there's no logic to bonus deals. However, if they happened to have excess of any one product, they just take some clear packing tape and slap it on to… just about anything. Here are some examples:

Toilet Paper 4-Pack with a Rubber Christmas Tree Ornament taped on front! Ah, a free Christmas tree ornament – just what I wanted to um, look at, while sitting on the toilet.

Head & Shoulders Shampoo PLUS a disposable razor! I'm using "Head and Shoulders" because I have a dandruff problem, but oh wait – I get a FREE RAZOR with it – to what? Shave my head with? (I must note that disposable razor blades are super expensive here, so this really IS a great deal, regardless).

Toilet Paper 4-Pack with a package of liquid laundry detergent taped on the front! Another thing I like to contemplate while sitting on the toilet – doing dirty laundry. (I'm starting to think that the "4-Pack of toilet paper" is just an easy thing for them to tape ANYTHING onto).

A can of RAID bug spray with a free Glade PlugIn taped on the front! THIS one actually makes *scents*! It's like bringing a bouquet of flowers to the roaches' funeral. Plus the Glade PlugIns are pretty pricey here, so this is another great deal.

When you see a deal like this, you need to scoop it up right away because more times than not, it's just a one-item deal (i.e. – there's only ONE can of Raid with the bonus Glade-PlugIn-gift. All the other cans of Raid on this shelf are by their lonesome).

Before we moved here, we knew we were going to be tightening the purse strings and decided to cut out all alcoholic beverages. This lasted two days (the amount of time it took us to get to a grocery store). Our first time in the store, we found ourselves walking down the wine/liquor aisle, when my dear husband proclaimed, "Ah, we should get some wine! Look, they have a one-liter box for just $5!"

Me: "But dear husband of mine… I thought we were giving up all alcohol forevermore?"

Greg: "Yes, but we should celebrate our arrival to Costa Rica! We are here! We did it!"

Me: "You have a point."

And this wasn't just any boxed wine – this brand was called "Clos" (made in Chile). Greg was already joking on and on about it:

"Just think, it'll be *Clos but no cigar*… close to a real bottle of wine, but no, it's just a box."

"Hey Jen, It's not *good* wine, *but it's Clos.*"

"Babe, look, *I'm coming out of the Clos-et.*"

He literally had me in tears from laughter. How could I say no to a $5 box of wine after that?

We thereby started our nightly routine of having a glass or two of boxed wine. It's not that bad, actually.

26. tico time

Even though Costa Rica is not an island (you'd be surprised how many people think it is), the people here live by "island time," or as they call it *"tico time,"* – a slower pace of life. Pura vida, the concept of Pure Life and not worrying so much, is taken quite seriously. Things will get done… mañana (which doesn't mean literally "tomorrow," but rather "whenever… no matter how many tomorrows it takes.")

We had read about tico time and also experienced it a little on our previous visit here, so we were not surprised when we saw it in action on a daily basis. We often saw it in restaurants and sodas – the servers take their time getting back to you with your beer, meal, refills, etc. Your glass may be empty for a long time, and unless you catch the server and ASK for another beverage, one will not be offered to you. All of the meals for your table may arrive at widely different times. We quickly learned, that when your meal is set down in front of you, and if you want to eat it while it is still hot, you dig in right away. This is not rude, as you never know when the other people will get their food.

The most important thing we've learned here is to just chill. What's the big hurry anyway? We've learned to enjoy our meal, and more so, our conversation with friends (or if we're alone, just each other). It's not the most important thing in the world to have our food right away, or at a perfect temperature, or to have our drinks constantly refilled – it's more important to enjoy life and each other's company.

I've also seen tico time on display at the post office. There is usually a line at the windows. There are three service windows inside, with the first window being the "Amway Window," where you can *only* pick up Amway products that you previously ordered. What is Amway doing at the post office? you ask. Excellent question! People who buy Amway here have a good deal, as there is NEVER a line at this window but there is always a teller – and you can just walk right up to it, interrupt the cute girl who is sitting there painting her nails, and get the Amway products you had ordered. The second window is usually closed. The third window is always open, and this is what the line out the door is for. Some people take a *very* long time at the window. Why? If you haven't already noticed, it may be the post office, but you can do so much more than just buy postage here – Amway anyone? People can pay for so many different things here, such as taxes, auto licenses, etc. (I'm not actually sure what they are doing – but they are not sending letters).

Surprisingly, when a person stands at the one available window doing their business for a long time, no one gets mad, or irritated, or bent out of shape. Everyone just waits pleasantly for their turn. There are even some chairs you can sit on, lined up against the wall, and like "musical chairs," as the next person gets up and goes to the window, everyone else moves over a chair. One advantage of tico time in the post office (or any other store, really), is that it makes you slow down, so that you begin to know the people who wait on you.

A gringa friend of mine told me this tico time story. She had met and made friends with a tico family and was invited to their house a few days later for coffee. On the appointed day and time, she promptly arrived at their house – no one was home. She saw them a few days later and they responded, "Oh yes, we were just returning from the store. We would have been there shortly." So they scheduled another day and time. My friend showed up, again on the appointed day and time, and this time her friends were home. After inviting her in, the family was in and out of the room chatting with her amicably – but it was obvious the coffee was not ready. About an hour later, there was a knock at the door – it was the wife's parents! It was apparent they were coming here for the "coffee" too. Another hour later (still no coffee or food) – *more* family showed up! Much, much later – they had a full sit down dinner, and the mysterious coffee finally appeared with dessert. The casual invitation to coffee had become a full day affair, a joyous event, including their new gringa friend and their extended family. My friend had never had so much fun nor felt so welcomed; and for her – that is the true value of tico time.

When we lived in Dallas, Greg and I were never, *ever*, late for anything. At least, not if I had anything to do with it. But now that we were in Costa Rica, retired, and living on tico time, I asked myself, what was the rush? Here was my license to slow down my life a bit and not live in the fast lane.

However, living on tico time *does* take some getting used to (and for some expats, this is an impossible task and they end up moving back to where they came from). When we lived in the States, I didn't particularly like the fast-paced, busy lifestyle, but honestly? I never thought about it; it was just the way things were. It seemed incredibly hard to just plain get together with friends or family – if they weren't busy with something, *we* were. I was determined to change my ways.

So, one day, when we were getting ready to go to a gringo happy hour, I mentioned to Greg: "You know what babe, we do *not* have to be the first ones there today. Let's branch out a little, and be a tad late."

"Jen, are you ok?"

"I'm totally fine honey, just trying to loosen up a little and live on tico time." Greg was very proud of me and agreed we should give it a try.

We had to watch the time just as carefully to make sure we were *not* on time, but we did it. We ended up arriving about 10 minutes late. Perfect!

We walked in and the happy hour was in full swing. We were probably the last ones to arrive for a change. Very cool!

Then the hostess, with a look of deep concern, ran up to me and asked: "Jen! Is everything okay? Are you alright?"

Me, confused: "Well, yes, we are fine. Why?"

Hostess: "You're 10 minutes late! I was worried about you!"

Sigh... I guess tico time doesn't apply to gringo events.

27. trips i've taken in costa rica

Within the first month of moving here, I took two trips all on my own. Both trips were unplanned.

My first trip happened the day I visited a local pharmacy (*farmacia*) for an odd spider-type bite on the inside of my knee. I had been bitten a couple of days earlier and the swelling was not going away. The bite hurt like heck and was starting to look infected.

Armed with our friends' directions, we went in search of a farmacia inside a mini-mall. As I was looking up at the signs, trying to locate the shop, I was unaware of the trough in the middle of the walkway. This trough is about a foot wide and is a 2" drop from the sidewalk, similar to the old-timey driveways made of two strips of concrete. Only instead of the friendly, soft grass, this trough was filled with gravel! The next thing I knew, I was sprawled across the ground, one knee embedded in the vicious gravel. It was *not* the knee for which I was already seeking treatment. Now I was in twice the pain.

If Greg and I had been totally alone, I probably would have cried. I don't do pain. But there was a tica walking behind us who saw me fall and was very concerned. I put on a smile and told her I was okay.

We walked into the farmacia and talked to a *farmacéutica* (pharmacist) about my spider bite. She looked at it very closely, asked questions, and then brought some topical cream for me ($16). The whole time we were there, the customer standing behind us and two other farmacia workers were talking worriedly in Spanish and kept pointing to my knee.

I looked down and saw a huge bloody mess. I let out an exclamation and the next thing I knew, two pharmacists had me sitting in a chair in a small room off to the side of the pharmacy. There was much excited talk as they thoroughly cleaned my wound, sprayed it with something, added a mysterious ointment, and finally taped gauze over it.

Another farmacia employee came up and joked to Greg in Spanish, pointing to me: "Ha ha, BOTH knees!" Yep, indeed, both knees were now messed up. Her effort to lighten my mood made me smile.

I had not even asked for help with my scraped knee and they treated me like a VIP patient. They wouldn't even accept money for their help. This is just one of many examples we have seen where the Costa Rican people are SO willing to help a stranger, even a gringa stranger. They don't think twice about it; it's just how they are. I later found out that most farmacias here have at least one doctor on staff. Many ailments for which someone in the States would go to a doctor or ER clinic for, can simply be taken care of at a farmacia in Costa Rica.

We were in a foreign country, could only communicate with a few Spanish words and hand motions, but we were still treated well. I walked away feeling cared for and loved. And there was no longer blood dripping down my knee, which was an added bonus.

My second trip also turned out to be unplanned.

I had made some Snickerdoodles, and decided to deliver them to a friend before Greg ate them all. I arranged a dozen cookies attractively on a pretty paper plate, then wrapped it in faux Saran Wrap, slipped on my best flip flops, and set off to walk the half mile to my friend's house.

It was a beautiful walk to her house and I enjoyed the perfect cool weather and the birds chirping – just another day in Paradise! As I walked up her gravel driveway, I caught a glimpse of the amazing views. I was relaxed and felt the breeze pick up. I lifted my head into the wind – my hair blowing off my face, sun shining down on me and warming me… .

Next thing I knew, I was sprawled out on the ground. Again. The SAME knee! And my cookies! They were scattered all over the dirt road! Seriously? I just wanted to cry. These were the last of my cookies, and they were meant for my friends!

I was almost at her house, so I picked myself up and put the dirty cookies back on the plate and kept going. I showed up at her door and knocked. She opened the door to find me babbling my head off: "I'm so sorry. I fell and all the cookies fell out and got dirty and are destroyed now!" Then she followed my gaze down to my bloody knee.

Good friend that she is, she whisked me inside, set me down in a chair and went to get first aid supplies – you would think she had once worked in a farmacia. She bandaged me up and then put the cookies in the freezer to give to some dogs for treats later.

Now, when you first started reading this chapter, I know you thought you were going to be reading about actual trips I took within Costa Rica. I'm sorry that I tricked you and made this chapter all about my being a klutz and taking falls instead. But bear with me – some real trips (er, excursions, shall we say?) are coming right up.

28. real trips

We have taken some cool trips since landing in Costa Rica – many of these purely by chance because of great friends we have or because one of our moms was here visiting (our opportunity to splurge and do touristy stuff!). Here are a few of my favorites:

Playa Jacó

Playa Jacó (*playa* means beach in Spanish) was actually our very first trip outside of Grecia. Everyone tells us Jacó is "not the best" of beaches in Costa Rica. It is known for its rough nightlife (prostitution and drugs), but we were just going for the day and were very excited to see the beach.

On the way, about an hour before we got to the beach, we came to a bridge over the Tarcoles River. The Tarcoles River Bridge is a popular stop for tourists heading to Jacó. Before the bridge, there are several tourist shops, restaurants, jewelry stands on the side of the road, and places to get *pipa fría* (they take a coconut out of a cooler, chop off the top, plop a straw in it and serve it to you – it's delicious!).

But the main attraction is looking over the bridge itself for a great photo op – 10-20 crocodiles hang out below the bridge. We weren't disappointed; the crocodiles were there! Just over the bridge, about 20 feet below, lounging on the muddy banks of the river. Pretty crazy if you think about it, I mean, they are just THERE – out in the open, not behind bars or anything.

Playa Jacó turned out to be awesome. Yes, it was hot, but there was a steady, cool breeze coming off the ocean, so it was quite comfortable, and we could cool off in the surf if we got too hot.

Greg and I took a short walk down the main drag of town, which was scattered with little shops, cafés, and hotels. He was happy to find a cigar store and bought a Cuban cigar. I found an adorable bracelet in a boutique – it was casual yet beautiful, with a bead pattern that looked like little daisies.

We enjoyed a great, laid-back, relaxing day. We rented beach chairs, which came with the use of a bathroom at the hotel, and hung out all day. It's a mystery to me how quickly a day at the beach can go by. We read, snoozed, watched the ocean, chatted, swam, walked along the shoreline, snacked, and walked some more. The day was over before we knew it. We tagged along with friends who had a car, and the drive was just a short hour and a half from Grecia. We had left early in the morning and were back home in time to see an amazing pink sunset that night.

Catarata del Toro (translated: "Waterfall of the Bull")

This waterfall is in the mountains of Bajos Del Toro Amarillo, Sarchi, Alajuela, and is purported to be the tallest waterfall in Costa Rica, but it is not known to many people. By the way – the purporting is done by the landowners of the waterfall.

I love hidden treasures, and this place truly seems to be in the middle of nowhere. We walked in through an open air restaurant with hummingbirds everywhere, paid the entrance fee, went through a gate at the back of the restaurant, and entered paradise. As we walked on the trail that would take us down to the fall, we caught glimpses of the waterfall through the jungle, and it was indeed tall and gorgeous. The trail we were on was level with the top of the waterfall, and separated by an extinct volcanic crater.

We continued on the nature trail through the jungle for about 500 meters before we saw the stairs that go down. LOTS of stairs. The trek to the bottom is not for the faint of heart. The stairs start as cement steps, but then gradually deteriorate into dirt steps, some being quite steep and slick with the moisture from the waterfall. There is not always a railing to hold onto. I thought the hike down would never end! By the time we reached the base of the waterfall, my legs were shaking like Jell-O.

However, all those steps were worth it! When we reached the bottom, we found a whole other world. The waterfall empties into a giant, old volcanic crater and is truly breathtaking. At the base it is very loud with a cool misty wind (which felt GREAT after that long hike down!). In addition to the large waterfall, there are smaller ones surrounding it. When we were there, the rock walls had a gorgeous array of rainbow colors, and there were boulders strewn around with patches of bright green moss completing this perfect picture. The river, crashing down over 300 feet into the tumultuous pool below, is an incredible sight to behold.

I stood there in peace and happiness for some time, taking in the powerful beauty of this natural wonder. Until it dawned on me that I had to go back up *all those steps*. So, upward and onward we went, stopping and pausing for breath after every few flights.

Afterwards, to stop our legs from quivering, we had a cold drink in the restaurant and watched all the hummingbirds. They seemed to be everywhere, hovering, flying from tree to flower, then buzzing by our heads. It was great to just sit, relax and listen to them "hum."

The Toucan Rescue Ranch

The Toucan Rescue Ranch is near San Isidro de Heredia, about 20 minutes north of San José. The best part about the Toucan Rescue Ranch is that they don't just rescue toucans! There are many different birds and animals here.

Leslie, the incredible owner and animal guru, was there to greet us and served as our personal tour guide. Down-to-earth, well-spoken, and open to questions, she clearly loves what she does.

Leslie's goal is to release each animal that is capable of sustaining itself back into its natural environment. A lot of research, including DNA testing, goes into determining the geographic location to which the animal should be returned after pinpointing its place of origin. In some unfortunate cases, however, either because the animal was domesticated or cannot fend for itself, it becomes a permanent resident with Leslie at the Toucan Rescue Ranch.

Although she showed us several different types of owls, Leslie explained that she had never "wanted" to rescue owls, but no other place would take them in. When people started coming to her door with injured owls, she couldn't say no – not when the alternative would be to let them die in the wild.

One of the permanent residents of the ranch is an oncilla, a small, rare feline similar to a margay and about the size of a large domesticated cat. Leslie quickly realized that it is quite docile (i.e., probably raised in a home), so it cannot be released into the wild. Leslie created an awesome environment for it, thanks to a generous donation from a couple staying at her B&B when the cat was brought in.

Leslie invited us in to take pictures of a large, beautiful barred hawk. When I questioned this, she told me confidently that the hawk would not fly out, as one of its wings is permanently injured. She said when this hawk first came to her, it was depressed and stayed in the corner and didn't fly around or do anything. Then one day, Leslie saw the hawk on the ground with its head down, and she was quite worried. On closer observation, she found it hunched over a snake! The hawk had hunted it, killed it, and then was jubilant and prancing around afterwards and has been happy ever since. She just needed a "job" to do.

Leslie ushered us into a porcupine's cage. I admit I was leery to go inside because I was pretty scared I would be shot with quills. However, once we entered, I could see the porcupine obviously ADORED Leslie. As soon as it saw Leslie, it came over to her and nudged her hand gently with its nose. And when Leslie offered it a fresh flower, the porcupine ate it right out of her hand.

And the sloths! We walked into several of the adult sloth cages, and they all reached out to Leslie with open arms. She is their momma, the one who raised them. It was so sweet to see! She even allowed us to pet them (on their backs, not their heads, which they don't like).

Leslie was raising two precious babies at the time we were there – a three-toed sloth and a spider monkey, which were the cutest animals I saw that day.

At the end of the tour, I tried to convince Leslie to let me take that baby sloth home with me, but she very seriously explained to me that it is illegal to have a sloth as a pet.

29. bank trips

There is one more kind of "trip" we have taken after first landing here in Costa Rica, trips to the bank to try to open a bank account.

Greg and I had decided to apply for Costa Rican residency, mainly because we didn't want to leave the country every three months, and also because we came here with all of our required paperwork that would expire six months after the notary/apostille stamp dates. Our very first visit to San José was to meet our new attorney, who had been recommended to us by friends. We handed over all our paper work, a hefty chunk of US cash, and he initiated our *rentista* residency process. There is another type of residency here called *pensionado*, but this required evidence of a monthly pension deposit (like social security), which we did not have.

Our attorney told us he'd call us once he received our "folio numbers," which were what we needed to *not* have to leave the country every 90 days, and also, would enable us to get finger printed and set up a bank account.

1ST TRIP TO THE BANK:

Once we were informed that our folio numbers had been issued, we headed back to San José to be finger printed and open our bank account. Our attorney mentioned that we would be doing this with Banco National. He had 15 years of experience working with them and assured us we would have no problems opening an account to satisfy the rentista requirements.

We arrived in San José with our driver-friend Wilson (we were not sure how to get there by bus), met with our attorney's assistant Randy The Runner, and proceeded to go and get finger printed.

After the finger printing, we went to Banco National, which was right around the corner from our attorney's office.

After going through the protocol of entering the bank, going through security, taking a number, and waiting – finally our number was called. We went over to a desk out in the open and Randy proceeded to talk in rapid Spanish to the bank clerk. She listened for a long time and asked Randy questions, and then all of a sudden, she started frowning, shaking her head repeatedly while speaking in Spanish to Randy. The only word we recognized was "NO."

Bottom line: the bank required a utility letter from the current place we were renting, even if it was in the landlord's name. Of course, this was something our attorney had previously told us we did NOT need. We went back to talk with our attorney; he told us this would be easy for us to obtain, and once we had it, we could try opening the account at the Banco National branch in Grecia. Sounded good to us – we would not have to make another trip to San José!

2ND TRIP TO THE BANK:

For our 2nd trip, we took our attorney's advice and went to Grecia with our utility letter in hand and with our tica friend who helped translate for us (thank goodness, because there was no English spoken!).

Our friend started by talking in rapid Spanish to the bank clerk. The bank clerk listened for a long time, and asked our friend several questions. Shortly thereafter, the bank clerk frowned then shook her head repeatedly while speaking swiftly. Again, the word "NO" was spoken frequently.

Bottom line: the Grecia branch had many, many more requirements, as they were not familiar with opening an account for the rentista residency. They requested all the documents required by the San José branch, and demanded, in addition, a letter from our attorney with detailed instructions about the CD along with three other letters! They were clueless about how to open this account.

We left, dismayed once again, and decided we would have to go to San José and require the assistance of our attorney.

3RD TRIP TO THE BANK:

For our 3rd trip, we went on the bus to San José with a gringa friend of ours (the bus is a great deal – $2.12 one-way per person). Our friend held our hands and showed us where to get off the bus, and how to get to our attorney's office from the bus. We meet with Randy The Runner at our attorney's office again and ran around the corner back to Banco National.

We were called over to a desk and Randy spoke to the bank clerk, once again. She listened, asked Randy questions… and then (again) there was lots of frowning, head shaking, and use of the word "NO." I had become quite used to this by now.

Bottom line: turns out *now* the bank requires a letter from our brokerage account in the States – saying that we have a large sum set aside and available for transfer, and also stating where our money came from so they can see if it is "clean" money.

We left upset. Greg, who was quite irritated at this

point, voiced his concerns to Randy, who relayed them to our attorney on the phone, and when we got back to our attorney's office – there was much apologizing. Our attorney said this is a new requirement, he had never heard of before, etc., etc., etc.

We contacted our brokerage guy in the States and outlined the letter we would need from him. He would send it through the mail directly to our attorney. Pura Vida!

4TH TRIP TO THE BANK:

Once our attorney informed us that he had received the broker's letter, we returned to San José via the bus – all by ourselves! (See, there is a silver lining in all of this!)

We met Randy at our attorney's office, walked over to Banco National and met with a banker again. Our story was explained as the banker listened patiently. And then – again, there was frowning. And head shaking. And rapid Spanish. Lots of "NO's." And this time, lots of pointing at our most recent passport stamps.

Then they called Randy into the back room and closed the door. Greg and I looked at each other. I started to seriously worry (visions of handcuffing and deporting were going through my head).

Bottom line: we were over the 90 day visa limit on our passports (even though our attorney told us we did not have to leave the country every 90 days because we had our folio numbers). We were "legal" (we would *not* be deported!), but this did not sit well with Banco National. They refused to open the account.

We left the bank hanging our heads. Randy tried to cheer us. But really, what could he say? He called our attorney, and he suggested trying a different bank, Scotiabank, just "a few blocks away." We agreed, and after walking about 15 blocks, arrived at Scotiabank.

We walked right in the front door– which was very UN-Costa-Rican. No triple door. No isolation booth or heavy security of any kind. I had my sunglasses on top of my head. No number to pull. Were we in the USA??

We were greeted right away by a banker named Andrew, who spoke kindly to us in perfect English, and Randy explained our needs. The banker escorted us into a private office and told us our options:

They could open an account for us if we had one of the following requirements: our cedulas, proof of ownership of property here, or proof of ownership of a corporation here.

We had none of these items, of course. Randy

explained that our cedulas were "in process," and that we had our folio numbers. Andrew said he would discuss this with his manager and see what they could do.

We didn't have to wait long. Andrew told us that if we could provide a utility bill in our name with our Grecia address, along with our 2012 tax return, they could make an exception and open an account for us.

Andrew gave us a list in writing, we made notes, he told us to call when we had these items and to make an appointment and they would open an account for us.

Even though our trip to Scotiabank ended in much the same way as our other trips to Banco National, we had more hope this time. We believed that if we actually provided the two things they requested of us (along with all of our other paper work), that we might just have a chance at getting a bank account.

5TH TRIP TO THE BANK:

Once we had all the correct paperwork, we made an early appointment with Andrew. He welcomed us back with a big smile and immediately escorted us into his office. I pulled out our paperwork – passports, driver's licenses, and multiple letters – and Andrew went to work.

A professionally dressed lady brought us piping hot coffee on a tray with condiments so we could relax while Andrew typed away on his computer. Every now and then, he would ask us questions or simply chat with us. He told us about where he lives (Cartago) and how beautiful and green it is. He showed us a picture of the volcano in Cartago, which was saved on his desktop.

Before we knew it (about an hour or so later) – VOILA! We had our account! We even had a debit card – with our names on it! And a pin number. And access to online banking. We could hardly believe it. All that was left was a simple wire transfer of funds and our business was done.

There was a certain "catch-22" in this whole "opening a bank account" experience of ours:

-To establish Residency (rentista), we needed to transfer a large sum of money into a Costa Rican bank account.

-However, to open a Costa Rican bank account, we must already be residents.

30. why we don't have a car

We do not have a car here. But every time we see a cute old Toyota Land Cruiser, those jeep-like ones from the 70's and 80's, my hubby ogles it and talks about wanting to buy one. They are everywhere here, and I have to admit they ARE cute. But then I think about paying for a car (even older ones are much more expensive here than in the States), plus the insurance, the annual inspections fees, the maintenance (which with something this old, driving on these pot-holed roads, might be an every day expense); and it's just not worth it.

And what is actually wrong with taking the bus everywhere? Absolutely nothing. Although there are a few small inconveniences:

1. It takes time, about 30 minutes to get to town (versus 15 minutes in a car), and of course we have to plan our schedule to catch the bus coming home. However, I have lots of time; I don't work a "day job" anymore.

2. Sometimes Greg doesn't have much legroom for his 6'3" frame.

3. It can be hot – mainly when coming home in the late afternoon with the sun shining down.

4. Walking around town is sometimes a little hard for me; I have to keep my eyes down and hold Greg's hand as the sidewalks here are *not* flat and I have a habit of tripping (as you now know).

Yet – the payoffs are huge:

1. We save money by not having a car. One-way bus fare per person into town is only $0.84; the gas alone to travel the nine miles from our house would cost much more.

2. We almost always see friends while walking around town everywhere (that is, if I happen to look up when my eyes aren't glued to the sidewalk). If we drove everywhere, this wouldn't happen as frequently.

3. We know our bus drivers. Even when we're not on the bus, they wave at us when they see us out hiking or sitting on our front patio.

4. We meet and get to know the people who live on our ridge and ride the bus, gringos and ticos alike.

Recently, for example, while sitting at the bus stop in town, we met four new people. The first, a friendly tica, chatted with us in Spanish and encouraged us by speaking slowly so we could follow what she was saying.

After she left, an older gentleman sitting at the bus stop promptly started chatting with us in English. He had retired here 5 years ago from San Francisco, California and was just loving life and couldn't help but tell us all about it. I don't think we got one word in during the whole conversation, but we enjoyed hearing about him and how much he loved living in Costa Rica.

Then, a sports car pulled up with two young men, and they yelled out the window:

"Hey, you guys look familiar! Are you Jen and Greg? We follow you and read your blogs!"

We chatted a bit and they offered us a ride.

So, true, we do not have a car and rely on the bus for transportation, but we could also take a taxi, hire a driver, walk, or hitch a ride with friends.

However, things *happen* when you take the bus. You have more time, so chances are, you will see friends, meet new people, or experience something new.

For now, I'm glad we don't have a car.

31. coffee picking

Costa Rica has two seasons – the rainy season (also known as the "green season" by marketing people) and the dry season. The rainy season usually starts in late April and lasts through November. From early December through mid-April is the dry season.

After the rains taper off, the coffee beans are ready to be picked. Coffee is one of the main exports with 90% of Costa Rica's coffee being exported. When Greg and I hike, we can tell when it's coffee picking season as all the coffee plants have bright red, glossy "cherries" on them. Starting in January, we see trucks full of coffee pickers on the roads going up the mountain ridges very early in the morning and coming back down in late afternoon.

Since 1982, the Costa Rican government has required all the coffee grown here to be "Arabica" coffee. Arabica coffee is a high-grade coffee bean. This type of coffee is produced at altitudes of approximately 2400 – 4500 ft. (so we are right smack dab in the midst of this, as we live at 4600 ft. and there are many coffee farms by our house).

The coffee cherries are all picked by hand because the coffee fields in Costa Rica are almost entirely on slopes and hills where mechanical methods would just not be practical. To ensure that all the cherries are picked at their optimal time, they are picked in multiple waves.

Typically, the coffee farms bring in workers from the neighboring country to the north, Nicaragua. The Nicaraguans (called *Nicas* by the locals) will work very inexpensively and stay here for as long as they need to in very humble and minimalistic houses. This is NOT a job to be treated lightly; these workers work HARD. They hike up and down hills all day long while carrying huge *canastos* (baskets) made of *bejuco* (a type of vine) to collect their coffee cherries – a huge workout for anyone.

They also wear very tall, durable boots. Why? Because the coffee fields are infested with spiders (tarantulas!), scorpions, and snakes of all kinds. Ack!

All this work is what goes into my morning cup of coffee. I love that I chose to live in a country that is abundant with coffee fields – they are beautiful and I enjoy the end result.

We have been on two coffee tours since moving here. One each time one of our moms was visiting. We did the Espíritu Santo Coffee Tour in Naranjo when Greg's mom (Shirley) was here, and then did the Britt

Coffee Tour in Barva de Heredia when my mom was here.

There was a stark difference between these two tours; here's my comparison of the two for you:

Espirtu: It didn't hurt that we were greeted by a handsome young tico named José, who turned out to be our guide as well. José greeted us as our van pulled up, helped us out of the car, and made sure we all had sunscreen and bug repellant. He then promptly escorted us inside ("don't worry about paying now") seated us at a table, and served us coffee as the four of us chatted a bit. We learned that as a boy he had grown up working in the coffee fields of Costa Rica (I admired him already!). We were fortunate to be the only people in José's tour and we got him all to ourselves.

Britt: We were not greeted by anyone; we paid and waited around until the specified time that the tour started. We did have a Dixie cup of coffee from a large thermos standing in the corner. At the starting time, we were herded into a large group (38 people!), and a woman started talking to us – switching between English and Spanish so fast we could barely keep up. Then two gentlemen interrupted her and it turns out they were part of the act. They took over, and yes they were very good actors and were funny, but you could tell this was scripted and intended more for a large group with a theatrical presentation.

Espíritu: After our coffee and chat, we started our tour by walking directly into a huge coffee farm. José explained about the coffee "cherry" (the red stage, when it is ready to be picked), and then he picked some and had us actually taste them, sucking on the sweet juice that surrounded the bean and then spitting out the bean. We never felt rushed and felt that we could take as much time as we wanted, taking as many pictures as we needed (and José was happy to take our picture, too!). We walked slowly through the coffee plantation while José educated us about the beans and allowed us plenty of opportunities to ask questions.

Britt: We were herded to the next location by the two gentlemen who continued to speak in their speedy combo of English and Spanish. They had some props which showed us different stages of the beans, etc., but to be honest, I just found it hard to concentrate on any information they were giving us. I felt like they were rushing through things too fast.

Espíritu: We watched a person actually roasting the coffee beans. José explained how there was a first "pop" of the beans when it reached a certain temperature, and then a second "pop." Timing was everything. The roaster-guru, wearing goggles, knew exactly when to open the hatch and let the beans out. Some were still popping as they spun in front of us!

Britt: There was a roasting machine standing there, but it was not in use. One of the tour guides stood by it with his microphone and explained the process. Then, he turned it on, and opened the hatch to let some coffee beans out. They were real coffee beans, but they had obviously not just been roasted. No popping going on here.

Espíritu: We were allowed in the production building and actually saw some beans being ground and prepared for packaging. It smelled heavenly! We were able to meet some of the employees who were packaging the coffee. They actually stopped the production line to give us their attention and to chat with us.

Britt: We were behind a glass wall, were not allowed to go into the actual production building, and they were closed that day – so we couldn't even see anything going on inside.

Espíritu: Shirley had her own personal escort service (José!). He was so sweet to "Churley" (what he called her), and every time we walked to a new spot, he gave her his arm and helped her walk. And I got to pour water over a REAL Chorreador (an authentic Costa

Rican coffee maker) in an old fashioned tico house. It was so cool!

Britt: We were herded into a theater with a stage where we were lectured to some more. After the lecture, they pointed to a few displays on the stage and showed a video (which they interrupted for more skits). I felt like I was in school.

Espíritu: The tour ended in their small gift shop where they served us several "mini" shots of coffee liquors and different types of coffee. We could take our time, experience the flavors and talk about them. José acted like he had absolutely nothing to do for the rest of the day. The coffee was made fresh just for us in a French press, and served by a cheerful young woman.

Britt: The tour ended at their *huge* gift shop where we were briefly told where the coffee, chocolate, and various other items were for sale. There were thermoses of coffee next to each type of coffee bean, and the coffee was good, although not always hot (and some thermoses were empty!). By the time I got through all the people to the chocolate wall, all the chocolate samples were gone.

I guess it's pretty obvious at this point that something just seemed to be missing for me at the Britt Tour. I'm more impressed these days with personable, smaller, laid back groups. Greg and I definitely learned and retained more information about the coffee process from the Espíritu Tour.

32. bartering

Before I moved here, I had read about bartering somewhere, and thought that it would be so cool to barter one of my "talents" for something I wanted in return.

Well, I'm happy to report bartering is alive and well, here in Costa Rica! I love bartering, especially because we are on a pretty tight budget. You just exchange something that you can provide that another person wants, for something that you want that the other person can provide.

Here's an example:

Juanita has chickens that produce several fresh eggs for her family every morning. Juanita also happens to be having problems with her computer lately.

Matthew is a computer/website master. Matthew also happens to love fried eggs for breakfast every morning.

How many eggs would it cost Matthew to work out Juanita's computer problem?

It's really that simple! Why exchange money when you can exchange talents or services instead? I just think this is the greatest thing.

One time we were returning from a trip to the States and were asked to "mule" something in from the U.S. for friends of ours. "Mule" is a term used by gringos, that really just means to fly something back from the U.S. to Costa Rica that you cannot find anywhere in Costa Rica (or that you can find here but it's *very* expensive). In exchange for our "muling" efforts, we were personally picked up from the airport at night (which is a 45 minute drive away and a hefty cab fare). Deal!

Another time, a friend bartered his homemade pineapple wine for a 9x13 pan of my homemade cinnamon coffee cake. Deal! His pineapple wine is really super yummy, and so much better than the Clos boxed wine.

Handmade bracelets for a handmade shirt? Deal!

Homemade apple pie for a few exercise classes? Deal!

Handmade éclairs for muling some products to us from the States? Deal!

You get the point. It's not always a perfect trade-off, but you'll typically barter again in the future, and if you weren't friends already, you might very possibly become friends. How great is that?

33. the simple life

Many ticos seem to have so much less than most North Americans. They do not make a lot of money and live on very little, yet they seem to be very happy. "Pura vida" is said often here, and "life is good" is the motto of many.

Here are a few examples of how the ticos live more simply. These things struck me as very odd at first, but now they make so much sense:

Raised garbage bins: Ticos do not spend money on garbage cans or trash barrels; instead everyone has a little "stand" near the road or they share one with their neighbors. This raises the garbage from the ground, and the cage around it protects it from animals. Simple, cost efficient, and it gets the job done. Also, Greg and I have noticed how much LESS garbage we produce living here in Costa Rica. In the States, we would empty our 13-gallon kitchen garbage can every other day. Here, we empty a 3-gallon recycled grocery bag just twice a week, mainly because we are eating less processed food with less packaging.

Baby changing table in a public restroom: Who needs a super-duper fold-down gourmet baby changing table like you see in the public restrooms in the States? In Costa Rica, you will usually find just an old folding card table with a simple "baby themed" plastic tablecloth over it. And really, this is all you need.

Solar water heater: Many tico houses do not have hot water. Some houses get hot water by leaving water hoses laid out on the roof with water in them and letting the sun warm them. Even if there is an electric or gas hot water heater, it is much smaller than one in the States. We have a three-gallon water heater, which gives us enough hot water for two long showers (sometimes more) and washing dishes once or twice a day. When I think of our house in Dallas having a 100-gallon water heater, I am amazed at the excess.

Solar clothes dryer: Most ticos only have a washer for their clothes. I take that back – they also have a dryer, a *solar* dryer. It is very common to see clothes hanging outside at all times. They are hung everywhere and anywhere: on clotheslines, draped over bushes, hung over the edge of the roof, and sometimes even laid out on the lawn. Whatever gets the job done, and it is so much cheaper on the electric bill. Actually, we use the solar drying system too, even though we *do* have an electric dryer. It uses so much less electricity (none!) and we have time. We just hang our clothes over our front porch railing and let them air dry. Smells so nice and fresh, too.

Solar hair dryer: I see ticas all the time getting on the bus with their long hair freshly washed and still wet. They brush it and fix it while on the bus... letting it air dry. No hair dryer needed here.

Living fences: There are several types of trees here that the ticos use for "living fence posts." These trees typically grow straight which works perfectly for this purpose. They plant these trees and attach the fence or barbed wire between them, and when the tree grows, it grows around the wire, encompassing it and creating a permanent fence post. Simple and effective.

Carrying a machete: Wouldn't life be easier if we all carried a machete around with us? Men and women, as well as boys and girls, are seen with them; working with them in the yard or on the side of the road, cutting down brush and even using them to cut the lawn. They walk down the road with them, or take them on the buses. Can you imagine if someone walked on the bus in the States with a machete? People would freak out and the police would be there in no time. Odd as it sounds here, it is just their way of life, and is not out of the norm to see a tico with a machete.

Living simply seems to be second nature to ticos. It works well for them, and Greg and I are striving to do the same… simplify our lives.

34. tico culture and español

Besides living simply and appreciating life, ticos are genuinely *nice* people. Most of the time if you ask the locals if they know any English they will say, "Oh no… just a little bit," but it's not true! They are quite modest. Once they start talking, they can carry on a whole conversation in English!

When we go to restaurants, we always greet them in Spanish, and try to converse in Spanish as much as we can. As soon as they know we are making an *effort* to talk in Spanish, they are helpful and sweet, and help us with the words and then they usually start speaking in English, which is even more helpful! It really amazes me, because here we are, foreign people living in their country, and they are kind and gracious to us.

Here are a few Spanish phrases I've learned to be helpful:

Buenos días: "good morning"

Buenas: this is a casual "hi" and you can say this at *any* time of day

Adiós: This is a casual greeting, which really means "hi and goodbye" – said in passing (even though in Texas we learned this only to mean "goodbye")

Hola: This means "hello," but is ONLY used here if you know someone well and are going to be sitting down and chatting further with them, not to be said in passing (even though in Texas we learned this as a greeting to be used all the time, not the case here)

Chau: (pronounced like the Italian word *ciao*) – a casual "goodbye" (I say this all the time)

Hasta luego: "see you later"

¿Cuánto cuesta?: "how much does it cost?"

Buen día: "good day" / "have a good day"

Muy rico: "tastes good" (like at a restaurant, if your food tastes good)

Tan amable: "you are so kind" (I love using this for people who go out of their way to be kind to me here, and it seems to be a huge compliment for them!)

Con mucho gusto: "you're welcome" / literally translated means "with much pleasure" (note: NO ONE says *da nada* here)

Mucho gusto: When meeting someone for the first time, "nice to meet you" (again, literally translated means "with pleasure")

My good friend Lair told me that most ticos are shy with people they don't know, but it is good for us as gringos to always greet people; otherwise if we don't say anything, there is a chance that we may appear as "frightened/anxious American tourists."

If you are a woman, after meeting a tico or a tica for the first time, the next time you see them, they will most likely give you a kiss on the cheek (one kiss, right cheek). A man will shake hands with another man. This "kiss on the cheek" custom is endearing to me, as it seems more personal than a hug. Even teenagers and little children do it, and I never get tired of witnessing this or being a part of it.

If a tico tries to sell you something, which happens sometimes in the park, it's better to not give an affirmative "no" or "no, thanks," but instead say *otro día* (maybe another day). In their culture, saying a point blank "no" is almost rude or offensive and it is hard for them to accept, so they don't give up or go away, but keep asking you again. It's like they can't take "no" for an answer.

Costa Ricans are also very hardworking; I have not met anyone here who is not. We always see people working in their yards or sweeping or mopping their front patios.

The tico babies and children are very well behaved. I have rarely heard a screaming tantrum anywhere in public. In the park, kids play together nicely and run around and have fun, but it never gets out of control. I'm not sure what the differences are exactly, but somehow the Costa Rican people raise their kids to be more respectful from a very early age. My friend Lair, told me he thinks one reason is because they hold their babies facing out (to see the world), instead of facing inwards. Food for thought.

We love getting to know the ticos and their culture; it has been an eye opening and very positive experience for us so far. It appears that the ticos truly LIKE gringos (or at least they like Greg and me!). We couldn't have picked a country with friendlier, warmer people than the ticos of Costa Rica.

35. a more permanent place

Before we knew it, our three-month lease at our landing place was rapidly approaching its end; it was time to start thinking about something more permanent. We had put the word "out there" in talking with neighbors and friends, to see if anyone knew of anything for rent.

Shortly after putting the word out (word travels fast here!), we started hearing from friends about potential places to rent. The first place we looked at was owned by a sweet tica and her Canadian husband, and we liked them upon first meeting them. The house they had for rent was really great. It was the last house on a short little road, at the bottom of the hill. Spectacular views, quiet, secluded, peaceful, nice back porch with two hanging swing chairs. Inside was also quite attractive, with three bedrooms, each with its own bathroom. But, it was huge. And it was only "barely" furnished. It was more space than what we needed and was on the high side of our budget at $800. So, we grudgingly passed.

The next house we looked at was a large house as well with two levels. The property was completely gated with cement walls and was very private. But we were only looking at the lower level to rent– the owner and his family lived upstairs and wanted to rent out the bottom part. The lower level was very dark inside and had two bedrooms, one bathroom, and no kitchen. However, the owner was going to "build us a kitchen – whatever we wanted." The place where the kitchen would be was actually beautiful, open, well lit and facing the backyard with an incredible view of the Central Valley. But the rent, at $700, was higher than we wanted to pay, and it seemed too risky to rent *before* this guy actually built the kitchen. Plus this gentlemen spoke no English, we spoke no Spanish, and we were afraid something might get lost in translation. Then again, it might have turned out to be a beautiful state-of-the-art kitchen, and in that case, we totally missed out on a good deal. We decided to pass on this opportunity as well.

It was getting closer and closer to the end of our three-month lease, and at the end of it, we were leaving for a two-week trip to the States, right at our 90-day mark. We'd either have to store our stuff with our current landlord or with our new landlord – if we ever found one. This was getting a bit stressful. Now that we were retired, we didn't want unnecessary stress in our lives. Greg kept telling me it would all work out, but I was getting nervous.

A couple of days after declining the "no kitchen" rental, a new tica friend called me. She had previously asked me what we were looking for and told me she'd keep her eyes and ears open for us. When she called, it was to say she had heard of somebody who might be interested in renting out his house.

I took the contact information and agreed to check the place out. Greg called the gentleman and set up an appointment for the next day (it was within walking distance of our current home). As we went into town later that day, we avidly looked out the bus window for the house he described to us. We saw it almost immediately, but it looked awful and very run down. I didn't hold out much hope for this one.

We were pleasantly surprised the next day when we found the correct house (NOT the one we had thought it was!), and it was lovely. It was on the main road, and the bus stop was just 25 meters from the front door. Open floor plan, two bedrooms and two bathrooms, almost fully furnished. Perfect for us! American style showers, toilets and kitchen. The woman even told me that the stove/oven was new, and she had never even used the oven. I couldn't wait to get in there and start baking!

It seemed too good to be true. We liked the gringo landlords, and at $600, the price was right. We shook on a deal!

Now that we had found our new, "more permanent" home, we were excited. More space, more privacy, a beautiful front porch where we could drink our coffee in the morning and watch the sunset in the evening.

36. my life as i know it

If you had asked me three years ago how I would feel about quitting my job in Dallas, selling everything I owned, retiring early, and moving to Costa Rica; I would have burst out laughing and said:

"Excuse me? What the heck are you talking about?"

Followed by: "Where *is* Costa Rica, anyway?"

See, I used to be like most people. I could not fathom retiring early and living in a foreign country. I could not even picture my life changing so drastically in so little time. Even now, looking back, it seems like everything happened incredibly fast after we made the decision to quit Dallas and move to Costa Rica.

In actuality, we gave ourselves over a year and a half to wrap things up and make the transition seamlessly and painlessly. This was my over-organized-type-A-planner-self taking over, but also one of the best decisions I made.

Now, if you had asked my hubby the same question three years ago, "How do you feel about quitting your job and entering early retirement, selling everything, and moving to Costa Rica?," he would have jumped off the couch and responded with:

"Let's go! I don't care *where* it is, I just bought us two plane tickets!!"

After ultimately making the decision that I was on board about moving to Costa Rica, I was oddly quite calm about it – probably because of my husband. Greg is truly my rock. When I get emotionally crazy or self-doubt has me running in circles, he keeps me steady, and pulls me back down to earth. His love and confidence in me has never faltered in the 20+ years I have known him. It helps that we really, quite simply, *like* each other. I just knew, with Greg – my rock, my gravity, my "realness" – by my side; I could do almost anything.

Not everything is perfect in Costa Rica. There are very large bugs (the Spanish catchall word for bugs is *"bichos"* – which I find comically appropriate). It takes forever to get anything fixed. Sometimes the electricity goes out for more than half a day without warning just because they're trimming trees down the road. It's sometimes hard not to have a car to rely on. I could go on, but I've trained myself to focus on the positive, not the negative. Negative things happen, surely, but I try to ask myself (or rather, Greg, will ask me):

It could be worse, right?

You're not in pain or dying, correct?

Surely, we can get by without a kitchen sink for a few days?

It was only a teeny tiny scorpion, and I killed it for you... .

So we don't have a washing machine for a couple of weeks, I'm sure we have enough clothes to get by for a few more days... .

This is better than having to work in the States, isn't it?

That last question always does it for me... even though my job in the States was not bad, I enjoy what I do with my time *now*, so much better. Was it crazy to quit my job and move to a foreign country? Sure! But with all the researching, organizing, planning and positive thinking that went into it – this huge life change has worked out for me rather well.

I never imagined myself as a "person living abroad," and yet – here I am! I've been in Costa Rica for a little over a year, and I've truly *never* regretted my decision.

Yes, things are different here; my life style has changed completely. Do I have as many assets as I had in the States? Nope. Do I have as much money as I did in the States? Absolutely not(!). Do I have gourmet restaurants, high-end shopping and concert venues here? Not so much (at least not in Grecia). Do I have money worries here? Sure.

And yet – my life is *richer*. Not in a material sense, but in a happiness-sense. What I do have is a husband who is free to spend all the time in the world with me. I have more opportunities to meet new people, explore a different culture, and build stronger relationships. I have the time to create healthy, delicious homemade meals that don't cost a fortune. I have a farmer's market open year-round with locally grown fruits and vegetables. I have a community where everyone comes out to celebrate on the street when the soccer team wins (and even when they lose!). I might not be able to afford an expensive gym membership, but everyday I hike along mountain roads that North Americans pay big money to see during a two-week vacation.

For me, less *IS* best!

Pura vida. Seriously.

THE END.

Or rather… *JUST THE BEGINNING*.

BONUS 1: recipes

Costa Rica Chica ~~Spanish~~ Costa Rican Rice

This is a wonderful, hearty addition to dinners here, instead of plain white rice. AND you can add shredded chicken breast or ground beef to make it a full dinner. Simply easy to prepare, I make this all the time.

INGREDIENTS:

2 TB vegetable oil
1 Tsp minced garlic
1 Cup uncooked regular rice
2.5 Cups water
1 small can of Maggi's *(U.S. folks can substitute one small can of tomato paste)*
1/2 small green pepper, chopped
1 small red tomato, chopped
1 Tsp salt (you may want more if you like salt)
1 Tsp garlic powder
a pinch of cumin

DIRECTIONS:

In a medium saucepan over high heat, add the oil and garlic, heat until sizzling, stirring frequently.

Add the rice and sauté for 2-3 minutes, stirring frequently.

Add the rest of the ingredients, stir to combine. Heat to boiling; reduce heat to low. Cover and simmer for 30 minutes, stirring occasionally, until rice is tender.

Serve with a little shredded cheese over the top… mmm mmm good.

Costa Rica Chica Bite-Sized Éclairs

These things. You guys. They are so cute, sophisticated and taste like heaven. Custard + chocolate + pastry? YES PLEASE! Your friends will think you are a gourmet chef! This recipe makes 12-14 bite-size éclairs.

INGREDIENTS:

Pastries:
1/4 Cup butter (cut up into pieces to melt easier)
1/2 Cup water
1/8 Tsp salt
1/2 Cup flour
2 large eggs (wisk together in bowl first, add as needed)

Custard:
1 1/4 Cups milk
3 large egg yolks
1/4 Cup granulated white sugar
2 TB flour (all purpose)
1 TB Maizena (fécula de maíz) (U.S.: corn starch)
1 Tsp Café Rica coffee liqueur (U.S.: coffee liqueur)
1 Tsp pure vanilla extract
½ Cup – 1 Cup whipped crema dulce (U.S.: whipping cream)

Chocolate:
A good semi-sweet chocolate (in a pinch, you can use chocolate frosting)

DIRECTIONS:

Preheat oven to 400°F (200°C).

In a small saucepan over high heat, combine butter, salt and water. Once the butter melts – bring to a boil and turn off heat immediately (as the water will evaporate).

Remove from heat and stir in flour until it forms a ball. Place in different bowl and add beaten eggs a bit at a time, mix until SMOOTH each time (you may not need ALL the egg!). You want a thickness so if you hold up spatula (facing down), the pastry sticks to spatula for a second, before falling down in a thick ribbon.

Place by small spoonfuls on greased baking sheet (or silpat mat) and bake for 25-30 minutes at 400 degrees, until just slightly brown on top.

While the pastries are baking, in a saucepan bring the milk just to boiling (just until milk starts to foam up).

While milk is heating, in a medium-sized heatproof bowl, mix the sugar and egg yolks together. Sift the flour and corn starch into the egg mixture, mixing until you get a smooth paste.

Once milk is ready, remove milk from heat and add slowly to egg mixture bowl, whisking constantly to prevent curdling. If you get a few pieces of curdled egg, you can pour through a strainer.

Then pour the egg mixture back into the saucepan (which you heated the milk in) and cook over medium heat until boiling, whisking constantly. When it boils, whisk mixture constantly for another 30 – 60 seconds until it becomes thick. Remove from heat and immediately whisk in the liqueur and vanilla extract. Cover the surface with plastic wrap to prevent a crust from forming. Cool to room temperature.

After custard has cooled, whip your crema dulce and fold into the custard with spatula, very slowly (you do not want to lose the whipped cream volume).

Melt chocolate in a double boiler.

To assemble your éclairs, use a serrated knife to slice the pastries in half. Spoon a large spoonful of the custard on the bottom half of the pastry. Take the top half of the pastry and dip just the top part in the melted chocolate, then flip over and place on top of the custard filling.

Store in refrigerator until ready to eat. ENJOY!

*NOTE: Want more Costa Rica Chica recipes?? Stay tuned for the **<u>Costa Rica Chica Cookbook</u>** coming soon!*

BONUS 2: what to bring if you move here

For those of you who are thinking about moving here, what should you pack? Keep in mind that we did not ship anything, and only brought nine suitcases with us when we first moved to Costa Rica.

We spent a great deal of time planning exactly what we needed to bring with us. Even though we knew we couldn't possibly think of everything, I think we did a pretty darn good job.

The best things we brought:

Our Apple family! Greg and I both have iPhones, iPods, Mac laptops, and I also have the iPad Mini.

The 4S iPhones work great here; after unlocking them we purchased SIM cards with minutes to use as local cell phones. We just re-load the minutes when we need to, about once a month for only $2 a pop.

As long as we have Wi-Fi, we can iMessage or Facetime our friends and family for free.

For me, one of the best gadgets on the iPhone is the camera – I use it all the time when I'm out and about.

It's so easy to whip out and get to the camera setting super fast, and it actually takes really good pictures.

The iPad Mini is also great, and I mainly use it as a reader with the Kindle App. We are both avid readers, and Greg has a non-Apple Kindle Fire (but he likes my iPad Mini better).

We don't have a TV here, but we watch movies on our laptops. We really don't miss having a TV at all! It's much nicer to take a walk outside or sit on our front patio and watch the world go by.

Other items we brought that we use all the time:

* Clothing: Flip flops, hiking boots, Crocs, Keens, tank tops, sun hats, shorts, and t-shirts. I also wear skorts all the time, which is a skirt with shorts built in underneath. So comfy and functional, and I can do a cartwheel at any time. Also merino wool socks are the best for hiking – they have natural wicking fibers and are very comfortable.

* Drug Store: Ibuprofen, Exedrin, Nyquil, Pepto-Bismol, Band-Aids, Neosporin, Insect Repellant (with deet), and good razors for shaving. And lots of sunscreen – sunscreen is very pricey here and is definitely something you need, as Costa Rica is only 10 degrees from the equator.

* Kitchen Products (remember, I love to bake): Kitchen Aid Mixer, coffee pot, crock-pot, coffee grinder, food processor, dutch oven, a good knife set (not Ginsu!) and Silpats (non-stick baking mats).

* Other miscellaneous items: Toolbox with some general tools, batteries, yoga mats, back packs, umbrellas. Oh, and reusable shopping bags! We use these all the time at the grocery stores. Especially since we don't have a car – these work great for toting groceries on the bus.

* Comfort items: two throws that are super soft and comfy and are easy to cuddle up in when it gets chilly out. Also, my Ugg slippers – when it's cold out, these just make me feel better.

* FRIENDS: Much to Greg's dismay, we brought all 10 seasons of DVDs of the TV show "Friends". This is my favorite TV show of all time, and I was not coming to Costa Rica without my friends.

* The Executioner: Given my severe bug phobia, I came to Costa Rica prepared. The Executioner lives up to its name. It looks like a tennis racket, but the racket part is electric. When you depress the button on the side, you turn the electric current on, thereby easily killing flies, wasps, and other small bugs. Of course I had bigger aspirations for

The Executioner and have since had the opportunity to use it on spiders and roaches (note: it may take more than one zap for larger bugs). If my first choice isn't available (Greg), The Executioner gives me an arm's length distance between myself and the bug. It gives me the power to... well, execute (amazon.com).

* Refrigerator magnets: We were worried about paper products and pictures getting moldy, so I had some of my favorite photos made into all different sizes of photo magnets that are plastered on our refrigerator. I love that I always get to see my friends and family that I miss (shutterfly.com).

Things we don't use or could do without:

* Too many jackets: You really only need one rain jacket and one fleece jacket. We are in the central valley at an altitude of 4600 feet, so it does get chilly sometimes.

* Rain boots: I brought these super cute rain boots because of the long rainy season, but have not worn them once. I prefer my croc's – I can get them wet and slip them off with no problem, and my feet do not overheat in them.

* Rosetta Stone: We had great hopes for furthering our Spanish language skills with Ms. Stone, but

this just never came to be. I can't say anything bad about Rosetta Stone – we never even opened the seal or took it out of its box.

* A purse: I brought a purse but never use it. Much more comfortable to use a backpack or an Aeropostale bag (like all the ticas do!).

Something else that didn't fit into any of our suitcases but we brought anyway: our sense of adventure and our sense of humor. Sounds dorky, but true. Both of these things have helped us tremendously to adjust to Costa Rica and to live here happily. Trust me, when I say this – these are two things you ABSOLUTELY need to survive here!

Good luck!

About the Author:

Jen Beck Seymour became the Costa Rica Chica in June of 2013. In her early 40's, she broke free of the rat race of North America where bigger was better, and moved to Costa Rica with her husband from Dallas, Texas. When she's not writing or blogging, she is either hiking, sipping coffee, yoga-ing, baking, making arm candy or enjoying a glass of (boxed) wine.

You can find her blog at: www.costaricachica.com

Thanks:

Heartfelt thanks go to my first Editor, Lair Davis, who after reading my first chapter told me, "Yep, you can write!" which helped me more than he knew. Lair only got through 10 chapters before he became ill and was diagnosed with an inoperable brain tumor; three months later he had passed away. With his zest for life, love of story telling, and constant smile – he enriched my life tremendously. I came to love him and miss him dearly.

Thanks to my second Editor, Caroline Harrison – you picked up where Lair left off with no questions asked, and dove in headfirst. You helped immensely to make my book a far better book. Thank you for showing me that sometimes less is more.

Thank you to Patrick Crinnion – you read an early draft with enthusiasm and offered valuable input.

Thank you to Nicholas Bradley – you came up with a better logo for me than I had imagined. I still love it every time I look at it!

Thank you to Fabiana Martínez and Bina Cline – your help before this went to the final paperback print were tremendously beneficial.

Thank you to my friend, Jeni Evans – you were one of those people who I liked upon first meeting (which doesn't happen often). Thank you for your kindness, your encouragement, and your unselfish help with the final proofreading. You helped me MORE than I can adequately express in words!

Thanks to my Mom, my biggest cheerleader – you endlessly root for me even when no one else does, not just about my book, but everything I do. Thank you for raising me in a loving, supportive and "you can do anything you want" family. I love you. PS – when are you visiting next??

And I saved the best for last, my Greg – this book would definitely not have happened without you. You are my true knight in shining armor. Thank you for your guidance, your wit, and your endless deletions of all my unnecessary parenthesis, ellipses and dashes… (oops – here's a few just for you). Thank you most for putting up with my less positive attributes, and no matter what, making me feel constantly loved and cherished. I love you with all my being. (Also, thank you for killing all the roaches and scorpions and spiders for me!)

Made in the USA
Columbia, SC
26 May 2018